STEALING
YOU BLIND

STEALING YOU BLIND

HOW GOVERNMENT FAT CATS ARE GETTING RICH OFF OF YOU

IAIN MURRAY

Since 1947
REGNERY PUBLISHING, INC.
An Eagle Publishing Company • Washington, DC

Library of Congress Cataloging-in-Publication Data

Murray, Iain, 1965-
  Stealing you blind : how government fat cats are getting rich off of you / by Iain Murray.
      p. cm.
  ISBN 978-1-59698-153-9
  1. Political corruption--United States. 2. Bureaucracy--United States. 3. Organizational effectiveness--United States. 4. United States--Politics and government. I. Title.
  JK2249.M87 2011
  364.1'3230973--dc22
                                    2011015464
Published in the United States by
Regnery Publishing, Inc.
One Massachusetts Avenue, NW
Washington, DC 20001
www.regnery.com
Manufactured in the United States of America

10 9 8 7 6 5 4 3 2 1
Books are available in quantity for promotional or premium use. For information on discounts and terms, write to Director of Special Sales, Regnery Publishing, Inc., One Massachusetts Avenue NW, Washington, DC 20001, or call (202) 216-0600.

Distributed to the trade by:
Perseus Distribution
387 Park Avenue South
New York, NY 10016

For Kristen

CONTENTS

PREFACE

Before I came to the United States in the late 1990s, I spent eight reasonably happy years working as a civil servant in the headquarters of the British Department of Transportation. At one point I even joined the National Union of Civil and Public Servants. It was a time of great change for the British civil service. Successive Prime Ministers Margaret Thatcher and John Major, having successfully privatized the great nationalized industries, were turning their attention to government itself. By the time I left my government job, the civil service was barely recognizable.

Then I moved to America. Literally the first thing I had to do was deal with American bureaucracy—the unlamented Immigration and Naturalization Service. It was everything British bureaucracy had ceased to be (not that British bureaucracy was perfect, I hasten to add)—arrogant in the extreme, driven by rules rather than by any sense of customer service, unresponsive and above all slow, glacial even. The slowness had a serious effect on me, as I was stuck for months after my initial work permit expired, unable to get a job and using up my savings (my payoff from the British government, as it happened). I recall at one point receiving a dressing-down from an immigration officer for missing an appointment. It turned out that they had sent the notification letter to my old address in Richmond, Virginia, rather than my new address in Alexandria, Virginia, despite them acknowledging they had received my change of address notification. I was upbraided for their incompetence.

Ever since that experience, I have been astonished at just how out-of-date American bureaucracy is. Its forms are incomprehensible, its procedures are mind-numbing, and its contempt for the people who pay its salaries is palpable. It appears to be driven by a simple principle: government of the people, by the bureaucrat, for the bureaucrat.

Yet I should stress here that the civil servants themselves, with several notable exceptions, have been decent, ordinary Americans I would be happy to have as my neighbors. Yet the system in which they operate almost forces them to disdain their fellow citizens. When you closely examine the system, it is one of legally sanctioned and enforced robbery.

Robbery can take many forms. It can take the form of plunder—simple expropriation of your property without so much as a by-your-leave. It can be extortion, where they take your property under threats of something bad happening to you. Or it can be a swindle, where you part with your property thinking you will get something in return and instead get far less or nothing at all. The American bureaucracy engages in all these forms of theft, and those who do the thieving are well-rewarded—at our expense. This book will expose how it's being done and identify the politicians, bureaucrats, and unions who perpetuate its being done—and what we can do to stop them.

Woodbridge, Virginia
February 2011

PART ONE

THIS IS
AL GORE'S HOUSE.
WHAT DOES
YOURS LOOK LIKE?

CHAPTER ONE

LIFESTYLES OF THE RICH AND POWERFUL

In their brilliant 2008 film *Not Evil Just Wrong*, Irish film-makers Phelim McAleer and Ann McElhinney present an interesting contrast between the powerful in America and the rest of us. They profile the family of Tim and Tiffany McElhany in Vevay, Indiana. The McElhanys live in a small house, but are putting away money for their dream house, which they're building.

The trouble is Tim's job at the steel plant is under threat from environmental regulations that are purportedly necessary to prevent global warming. At the end of the movie, Tiffany drives to Nashville to deliver a letter to former vice president Al Gore, the main proponent of such regulations. In contrast to Tiffany's modest home, Gore lives in a vast mansion.

What makes this more interesting is that Gore's resume is one of what is euphemistically called "public service." From Harvard, Gore served as an Army journalist in Vietnam for four months before returning in 1971 to spend a few years bouncing between divinity school, journalism, and law school, which he entered in 1974. He failed to complete law school, being elected to the United States Congress in 1976. From there he went on to serve successively as congressman, senator, and vice president of the United States, until his seemly progress along the *cursus honorum* was cut short by the electorate and the United States Supreme Court in 2000. Since then he has made a living lecturing and investing in green technologies for which he is a de facto lobbyist.

So Al Gore's mansion was essentially paid for by the taxpayers of Tennessee and the United States, who supplied his salary as a "public servant." He had no other career to speak of, and certainly had never worked in a steel plant. When Tiffany McElhany drove through the front gates, she probably had no inkling that she and her husband were contributors to the Al Gore mansion fund.

Gore's residence is a twenty-room mansion near Nashville, Tennessee. It has two wings and a large outdoor pool, spaciously set in lushly wooded grounds with a circular driveway and extensive parking space. Type "312 Lynnwood Boulevard, Belle Meade" into Google or Bing maps and you can bring up a satellite picture of the place. That's Al Gore's house. What does your house look like?

Gore is not alone. In fact, his partner in the White House, President Clinton, has an astonishingly similar resume. While coming from much humbler roots than the patrician Gore, Bill Clinton was also the beneficiary of a political career. Indeed, he set his sights on this at an early age, as he relates in his autobiography, *My Life*:

> Sometime in my sixteenth year, I decided I wanted to be in public life as an elected official. I loved music and thought I could be very good, but I knew I would never be John Coltrane or Stan Getz. I was interested in medicine and thought I could be a fine doctor, but I knew I would never be Michael DeBakey. But I knew I could be great in public service.[1]

Clinton went straight from Hot Springs, Arkansas, to the Georgetown School of Foreign Relations in Washington, D.C., then to Oxford as a Rhodes Scholar, then to Yale Law School, where he began dating Hillary. He left Yale in 1973 and became a professor at the University of Arkansas. He ran for the House of Representatives in 1974. Despite being defeated, he stayed the course and was elected Attorney General of Arkansas in 1976, only three years out of law school. From then on, it was relatively smooth sailing to the governorship and the presidency. While Gore had at least briefly been a journalist after leaving Harvard, Clinton had no job that wasn't financed by the taxpayer until he left the White House. Yes, we probably paid for that cigar, too.

Gore and Clinton are not the subject of this book, but they are emblematic of the government leisure class this book is about. They represent the epitome of the "public servant"—people who make a frankly extraordinary living by supposedly working for the rest of us, but actually by putting endless, petty (and not-so-petty—sometimes career-threatening and liberty-endangering) bureaucratic obstacles in our way.

As we'll see, most public servants, while not as well-endowed as Clinton and Gore, are far better off than Tim and Tiffany McElhany. They have salaries, benefits, and powers that make them part of a cushy and coddled economic stratum. Despite the global slump since 2008, these are boom times for them, and the easiest way to see that is to go to where they live, in the suburbs of Washington, D.C.

America's Wealthiest District

Where is the wealthiest congressional district in America? Beverly Hills? No. Manhattan? Think again. It's actually the 11th District of Virginia, made up mostly of the outer Washington suburbs in Fairfax County and Prince William County, which is where I happen to live. According to a survey by *The Hill* newspaper in 2006, using data from the 2000 Census, the district has a median household income almost double that of the average district—$80,397 compared with $41,994.[2] The reason for the district's affluence, says Claremont McKenna College professor Frederick Lynch, is "because of the presence of high-level federal workers and two-income families." Needless to say, many of those two-income families have both members working for the government, either directly or indirectly. And remember, those data come from before the financial crisis, before the massive stimulus spending directed largely at government employees, and before the rapid rise in government salaries we'll examine later.

To take a look around Virginia's 11th District is to see an island unaffected by the economic tsunami unleashed by the financial crisis. The houses are, for the most part, pleasant single-family homes or townhouses built comparatively recently. That's because the population has boomed. Fairfax County's population has increased by 200,000 people since 1991, while Prince William County has added 84,000 residents since 2000.[3] The top three employers in the county are the county's public schools, the federal government, and the county government, accounting for 50,000 employees between them, up 10,000 from ten years ago.[4] Many of those not working directly for government are working for semi-governmental employers like Freddie Mac (up to 7,000 employees) or government contractors like Northrop Grumman or the management consultant Booz Allen (up to 10,000 employees each). All these employers pay well.

More to the point, they continue paying. It is received wisdom in these parts that the area is "recession-proof," thanks to the main source of income being the government budget. This shows in the unemployment rate. In September 2010, the national unemployment rate was 9.6 percent across America. In Fairfax County, Virginia, it was just 4.6 percent, less than half the national rate. Fairfax is a good place to get—and keep—a job.

The resilience of the national capital area thanks to government funding is obvious in another area as well. Home prices in the area have not decreased by nearly as much as they have in the rest of the country. Indeed, home prices are still around 75 percent higher than they were in 2000, even if they've decreased from the peak of 150 percent higher in 2006. That's a better performance than any other area in the nation. Moreover, they started increasing when other areas were still on the downward slide. As Tim Iacono of Iacono Research points out, "The change in fortune for Washington area home prices began when the bailouts/stimulus began in earnest (i.e., late-2008/early-2009) and, in recent months, the home price index is further separating itself from all others."[5]

In other words, back when the rest of the nation was being told that bailouts were the only answer to America's financial ills, when arms were being twisted in the halls of Congress with more than usual viciousness to ensure the passage of a stimulus bill, and when America was voting for both hope and change, one of the main effects was to ensure that people who worked for Freddie Mac did not see the value of their homes collapse.

Freddie Mac, by the way, is a generous employer. In 2007, the government-sponsored company paid its Chairman and chief executive, one Richard Syron, a whopping $19.8 million in various compensation guises. That was the year Freddie Mac's stock value halved as the company's role in the gathering mortgage crisis became clear. The company continues to pay handsomely. A quick look at the CareerBliss website will tell you that the average advertized salary for positions at Freddie Mac comes in at $89,000, compared to an average of $46,000 for other companies in the financial services industry. Director salaries are over $120,000. Even after Freddie Mac was bailed out by the taxpayer, its new head, Charles Haldeman Jr., was paid more than $6 million in 2009. The Federal Housing Finance Agency said the salary was justified in order to "attract and retain" top talent.[6]

Top talent is plentiful in Fairfax County, if the possession of a bachelors' degree indicates talent (and, as we'll see later, that may no longer be the case).[7] In 2008, almost 60 percent of Fairfax County adults possessed such a degree; the national average is just under 25 percent. Yet a disproportionate number of these talented people work to find innovative ways to remove cash from taxpayers and direct it to their own salaries and house prices. Not one of the top ten employers in the county is a wealth-generating industry; they all live off the taxpayer.

Even Washington, D.C., itself, such a symbol of urban decay that it became America's Murder Capital in the 1990s, bounced back as government grew. In December 2010 it was announced that Washington now had the highest median income of any major city, and that housing prices had grown there by over 5 percent, even as the rest of the nation's declined by 3 percent. The average business rent there was now higher than the average rent in New York City, and the city finally found a booming business in recession: journalism, because industries needed to know what new laws and regulations the government had planned for them.[8] Of course new government workers flooding in meant a change in the demographics of the city. In March 2011, the Census Bureau announced that African Americans made up less than 50 percent of the city's population for the first time since the 1950s.[9]

The New Robber Barons

Jack Johnson followed a familiar career trajectory: law school to academia to bureaucrat, working as an attorney for the IRS. Along the way he made important political friends, which helped him become State's Attorney and County Executive for Prince George's County, Maryland, which is just outside Washington, D.C., and not coincidentally is the wealthiest majority African American county in the nation, with 834,000 residents and a median income of $71,696. The Prince George's County website praises its own, saying that its State's Attorney issued a message that "was loud and clear—no one was above the law."

Jack Johnson, however, might have been an exception to his own message. Allegedly, for several years Johnson had been receiving payments from one unnamed developer to help him obtain federal, taxpayer-funded grants via the County's Department of Housing and Community Development to build "affordable housing."[10]

On November 12, 2010, however, the developer was wearing a wire, and their meeting this time was under surveillance by the FBI. (The developer, it appears, had been caught by the FBI and had agreed to help them.) The developer gave Johnson a check for $15,000 in return for Johnson's "using his official influence and authority for the benefit of [the developer] and his companies." FBI agents then entered the room and asked about the payments. Jack Johnson explained that it related to a party to mark the end of his time as County Executive.

FBI agents also visited Johnson's home. His wife called him asking what to do. His cell phone was monitored by the FBI. Johnson told her not to answer the door but instead to go to "his drawer" where she would find a check from the developer. His wife asked whether she should get the "cash out of here too." Johnson told her, "Put it in your bra or something...." When she found the check, believed to be for $100,000, she suggested flushing it down the toilet. Johnson agreed. FBI agents found $79,600 in Mrs. Johnson's underwear (she had followed her husband's advice to the letter). Mr. and Mrs. Johnson were both arrested.

Just a few days later, on November 17, 2010, undercover reporters for TV channel FOX 5 D.C. met with a real estate agent at 2:00 p.m. to view a house in the county. The agent also happened to be deputy director of the Office of Human Relations Commission. At a salary of $106,000 a year, he was responsible for investigating complaints of discrimination made within the county. This did not stop him from selling houses during the workday, as he explained to the reporters:[11]

> FOX 5: "I hope we're not pulling you away from anything too important."
> Man: "Don't worry about it, bro. I just work for the county when I ain't doing this."
> FOX 5: "Is this a part-time gig for you?"

Man: "Well, yes and no. Um, with real estate and the Internet, you can do everything anytime and I have total flexibility on my job, so…"
FOX 5: "Oh, alright."
Man: "I'm Deputy Director for the agency, so…"
FOX 5: "Ok."
Man: "Affords me the flexibility. If you need me, y'all call me on the cell. I'm out."

According to the reporters, the deputy director's entrepreneurial behavior was well known around the office, as was the fact that he used a county car while selling real estate. On the day in question, he clocked in for a full eight hours' work with the county.

Informants within the office also pointed to his boss, the executive director. One employee claimed that on a typical workday, "She may not come in at all. She may come in at about eleven or one o'clock. Stay an hour or two. Leave." The TV station reporters tested this by sitting outside her house on three days when the county confirmed she had clocked in. Her county car "never moved."

When most people think of a public servant, they think of a post office worker: unimaginative, slow, and poorly paid. But today's public servants are very well paid—and they have accrued power and wealth by making themselves essential regulators of private sector business—while still retaining the leisurely working pace of their predecessors.

The typical "public servant" enters the bureaucracy at a starting salary of $75,000, less if she's a payroll clerk ($50,000), more if he's a firefighter ($100,000). Assuming no extra raises, performance bonuses, or promotions, after thirty years he'll be making in real terms $117,000 (thanks to seniority). He'll also have a generous, guaranteed pension scheme, perhaps without any contributions on their part (because we'll pay for it when they retire), in contrast to the rest of us who have to carefully save in a 401(k)—and risk the vagaries of the market, too.

That's *the baseline* for the least imaginative (or most honest) bureaucrat. The ones who expand their bureaucratic empire, or help their labor union, or invent new ways to shake down taxpayers and businesses can do even better. One deputy police chief in San Francisco, for instance, made more than half a million dollars in his last year before retirement.

Public sector workers—the public servants—make one and a half to two times as much as their private sector colleagues who perform equivalent jobs and who pay the public servants' salaries. And that's not counting the more generous benefits and leave arrangements public sector workers have.

The best bureaucratic empire builders can, like Jack Johnson, get the ultimate prize—appointment or election to high office; and their friendly public-sector unions can raise the cash and provide the block votes to keep them in office.

That's just the beginning. What makes these officials robber barons is their extraordinary degree of power over us. Businessmen have to provide us with goods or services we want, or they go out of business. (In that sense, the private sector is truly full of "public servants.") Bureaucrats, however, just order us about, threaten us with jail if we don't comply with their self-aggrandizing regulations, and then have the gall to tell us we should be grateful to them.

America's government class has radically different interests from the rest of us—and it uses the power of government to further those interests. As J. P. Freire, writing for the *Washington Examiner*, put it, government today is "not so much about haves and have nots. It's about haves and *have yours*."

CHAPTER TWO

GOVERNMENT 101

Madison, Wisconsin, early 2011: a governor facing a budget crisis realizes that lavish government worker compensation deals are bankrupting the state. He was just elected to put this position right, so he moves to restructure these deals with the aid of the newly elected state legislature. The workers and their unions object. Democratic state senators flee their responsibilities, the capitol, and even the state, delaying passage of the budget bill. Unions, aided by their out-of-state comrades and President Obama's Organizing for America campaign group, bus in thousands of supporters to storm the state capitol. State police appear to allow the protestors access with only minimal opposition. The union supporters flood onto the Senate floor and throng the balcony. They chant, "This is what democracy looks like."

In fact, this is what modern government looks like.

Modern government serves itself; it has grown enormously, and its goal is to preserve and extend the powers and privileges of politicians, bureaucrats, and public-sector unions.

A good example of how modern government works might be the "Bill with No Name" of 2010,[1] a $26.1 billion bailout for the states. The biggest part of the bailout was an "Education Jobs Fund" that was essentially a $10 billion slush fund for unionized teachers, like those who were the main target of Wisconsin Governor Scott Walker's reforms— paid for by slashing $12 billion from a food stamps program. Now, food stamps might themselves be a bad idea, but is subsidizing public sector workers a better one? It is if you're in government.

Madison Would Turn in His Grave

The Wisconsin affair showed that government workers form a spoilt, over-privileged elite class that takes money from taxpayers as if it was some feudal right, and which reacts to genuinely democratic attempts at reform with contempt for democracy. Government resorts to thuggery, intimidation, and obstruction when it fails to get its way. Those tactics can be aimed at the individual citizen and duly elected governors alike. When government succeeds, it divides the spoils among its supporters. When it fails, it retreats, goes into hiding, and then emerges again to attack once more.

What Governor Walker was trying to do was simple. He faced a hole in his budget of over $3 billion. Wisconsin's teachers (teachers are by far the largest block of government employees in any state) had some exceptional privileges. Governor Walker's proposed budget required government employees to contribute 5.8 percent of their pay to their pensions and to pick up 12.6 percent of their health care costs. The bill also gave workers the right to say no to a union if they don't want to join. State employees currently are required to pay union dues simply to keep their jobs, even if they aren't members of the union. The bill also took away the union privilege of automatically deducting money from workers' paychecks.

For this, democracy was upended as the teachers, their unions, and their allies launched a virtual coup d'etat to stop Governor Walker from doing what he was elected to do. (We'll look in detail at the role of the unions in Wisconsin and why they were so angry in chapter seven of this book.)

The story gets more outrageous when you find out just how much Wisconsin teachers are paid. The average personal income in Wisconsin is $37,398 a year, according to the Bureau of Labor Statistics, part of the Department of Commerce. The average teacher earns $49,580 in cash wages for nine months' work a year. Benefits—the reason for the fight in Wisconsin—increase that by another 52 percent, because the average worth of health insurance, retirement benefits, and other insurance benefits is $26,005. So a household where both adult members are teachers—not an uncommon occurrence—is earning over $150,000 a year in salaries and benefits, plus three months' time off work. It's a sweet deal whichever way you look at it. (We'll look more at government benefits—and the pay of teachers in particular—later in the book.)

We pay for all of this. Government workers all over the nation are enjoying a better standard of living than the people who are paying them. That represents a significant breach of the old "social contract" whereby government workers, when they were public servants, earned less than their private sector counterparts but made up for it in better working conditions. Now they still have the better conditions, but they also have better pay. It's a slap in the face for the taxpayer—and remember that the taxpayer is, nominally, their boss.

Our New Leisure Class

The government-employed teachers who are paid handsomely for nine months' work a year (private sector teachers earn much less, please note) are a great example of our new leisure class. Previously, the leisure class consisted of aristocrats existing parasitically off the backs of the rest of us. The fact that our new leisure class comprises government workers shows that nothing much has changed. We frequently pay our government workers substantial sums to do little or nothing.

Take the case of one Washington, D.C. firefighter, who was literally paid two years' wages for nothing. In 2008, Natalie Williams, a twenty-year veteran paramedic firefighter, sent an invoice for CPR training for the princely sum of $120 to a Business Improvement District.[2] The invoice was on official stationery, but instructed the client to pay the money directly to Williams. In private industry, this would have been an on-the-spot firing offense. In the D.C. fire department, Williams was placed on administrative leave while her case was investigated. For the past two years, Williams has continued to receive her $72,000-a-year salary while the residents of D.C. get nothing back from her. As we'll see in chapter eight, government-employed firefighters are paid for sleeping on the job, but this takes the cake.

Then there was the Boston police lieutenant named Matthew Spillane who, through judicious use of overtime, managed to make $272,000 a year. That would be astonishing enough on its own, but early one morning when he was clocked in for an eight-hour overtime shift directing the towing of vehicles around the city, he accidentally discharged his police-issued weapon. At home. Again, you'd expect some sort of repercussion for this behavior, but according to the *Boston Globe*, Spillane was never even disciplined.[3]

Even when government does attempt to discipline its employees, it often finds it cannot. There was one government worker in Arizona who had lied to state officials and violated personnel policies (in pursuit of a romantic affair). He was fired, reinstated after a lawsuit (even though he admitted lying and violating personnel policy), fired again for lying and neglect of duty, and then reinstated (and granted $170,000 in lost pay and benefits) because the second charges constituted "double jeopardy"![4] If an employer has no effective disciplinary sanction, then employees have no real incentive to do their jobs. The expression "close enough for government work" derives from precisely this problem.

We also pay extravagant pensions to former government workers who decide they've had enough of sitting around the office all day and would prefer to sit around at home. All over the country, government employees get sweet deals like those of Wisconsin teachers in the shape of free or low-cost pension plans. This led one private sector worker to write to John Derbyshire of *National Review*, pointing out that investment advisers had told him he would need $1 million in the bank for every $20,000 he'd want to live on annually in retirement. So to get the same sort of deal a public employee would get, he'd need to save up $2 or $3 million. He saw little chance of achieving that, particularly because "I have to pay about half of everything I make to the government in no small part so that the average public employee can live better in retirement than I'll ever have the chance to dream about."[5]

Bearing the existence of this new leisure class in mind, it's important to recognize just how much of our economy we have entrusted to this class. The answer should be enough to make you faint.

Government by the Numbers

America spends a vast amount on government, and that sum is growing like Topsy. Most of our government spending is, ultimately, at the federal level. When it comes to the size of the federal government, you can't go wrong with Brian Riedl's *Federal Spending by the Numbers*, published by the Heritage Foundation. It's a handy and very visual guide to just how much money the Feds spend—and waste—every year. Most of the spending figures that follow can be found there, although ultimately they derive from the Office of Management and Budget (OMB) and the Congressional Budget Office (CBO).[6]

In 1990, the federal government spent (in 2010 dollars) a grand total of just over $2 trillion. In 2000, that had grown to just under $2.3 trillion. By the time George W. Bush left the White House, federal spending had ballooned to more than $3 trillion. Barack Obama pumped federal spending up to an astonishing $3.6 trillion for 2010.

How big is a trillion? It's staggeringly huge. You could spend a million dollars a day for two thousand years and still not spend a trillion dollars. Or consider this: "1 million seconds is about 11.5 days, 1 billion seconds is about 32 years while a trillion seconds is equal to 32,000 years."[7] That's the scale of spending we're talking about—almost literally unimaginable.

Moreover, today about a third of the vastly inflated federal budget is financed by borrowing. George W. Bush entered office with a budget surplus of $302 billion. He left office with a deficit of $467 billion. President Obama's 2010 budget included a deficit of *$1.5 trillion.*

And the trend is upwards. By 2020, federal spending is projected to reach $4.7 trillion. While the OMB reckons that tax revenues will grow—with the Feds raking in $3.7 trillion in taxes—that still leaves a deficit of $1 trillion, more than double any deficit before 2008. And remember that these figures are all adjusted for inflation, and that they'll undoubtedly get worse. Spending has exceeded inflation by 19 percent since 2008.

Most people put this spending increase down to pork, but pork is not the problem. Sure, it's *a* problem, but in reality it's quite small beer. In 2005, when pork was at its height as the Republican-controlled Congress lost its way, the budget contained 14,000 pork projects, but they only cost $30 billion. Public outrage has already reduced that figure to about $16.5 billion, and it would be great to get the figure down to zero, but pork is just a drop in the bucket of federal spending.

The fact is that most of the inexorable rise in spending is driven by entitlements—Social Security, Medicare, Medicaid, and the like—the costs of which more than doubled between 1990 and 2010 (when they went over $2 trillion). Another factor is the interest we pay on the national debt, about $200 billion now, but sure to jump soon.

Discretionary spending is now about $1.4 trillion.[8] You might think a lot of that is driven by the "war on terror," and it is, but while defense and security spending has increased by 51 percent since 1990, spending on discretionary domestic programs has jumped more than twice as much and with far less excuse. When people say that Congress has been spending like a drunken sailor, they forget that a drunken sailor runs out of cash and has to sober up. A congressional sailor, however, seems to have a credit card with no limit.

Here's a good example of how that works. Back in 2000, tax revenue was running at about 20 percent of GDP. The three biggest entitlement programs—Medicare, Medicaid, and Social Security—were between them running at about 7.4 percent of GDP. According to the CBO, however, those three programs, especially Medicare, are projected to soak up 18.4 percent of GDP by 2050. In other words, in about forty years we won't be able to pay for anything else—no Army, no post office, no welfare, no renewable energy subsidies, or anything else—without significant tax increases.

How big a tax increase? The Heritage Foundation calculates we'll need to raise an extra $12,000 per household. That figure assumes that other government programs won't grow (quite an assumption), and is adjusted for inflation *and* income growth. Bear in mind that the average family earns $42,000 a year, and pays $16,500 of that to the feds. By 2050, according to what seem like rosy estimates, we'll be sending almost half our paycheck to the IRS—and that's before the payroll tax and any state or local taxes take their bite. As we'll see in the next chapter, the IRS has plenty of ways to force you to pay—up to and including at the barrel of a gun.

Entitlement spending as a whole is 56 percent of federal spending and is on autopilot to keep on growing. Anti-poverty measures have been a big winner recently. In 2000, we spent under 3 percent of GDP on them. Now we spend about 4.5 percent, and spending on these measures has increased 89 percent faster than inflation in the past decade. Medicaid and food stamp enrollment has increased by 20 million in that time period, with the benefits also increasing faster than inflation. In the warped thinking of government types—and this is something we'll return to time and again—this is a sign of success. The statement "We are spending now more than ever on [insert name of program]" is a badge of honor for any bureaucrat or politician. Yet it's actually a sign of failure. Spending more to help more people is not a sign that the program is working, it is a sign that it is failing to address the ill it is meant to cure, whether that be poverty, obesity, insert your cause here.

Then there are the programs that are popular and will remain popular until we change our national way of thinking about them. K through 12 education is a case in point. Most people these days believe that the federal government has a role in education—and federal education spending has jumped from $18 billion (in today's dollars) in 1980 to $86 billion under President Obama. Spending on veterans is a similar story: the federal government spent $54 billion annually in 1980 and is spending $124 billion today in inflation adjusted dollars. We'll look at the supposed justification for these discretionary programs and the reasons why most of them just impose costs on our economy in chapters four, five, and six.

This astounding growth in entitlement spending is one reason why a majority of Americans now gets some income from the government. In fact, we are now taking marginally more in welfare than we pay in taxes (about $2.1 trillion each). The economist Gary Shilling, who measures how many Americans get "significant income" from government, says that in 2007 (the last year covered in his analysis) almost 53 percent qualified for that label. In 2000, the figure was under 50 percent. In 1950, it was just 28 percent. Entitlements have made us much less self-reliant as a nation.[9]

And it's not just the spiraling costs of the programs, but the fact that we have to borrow money to pay for them. If President Obama gets his way and spending remains at the levels he wants, then the national debt will be at an astonishing 90 percent of GDP by 2020. We're currently paying $209 billion annually in interest costs. That will balloon to $760 billion a year by 2020. Interest costs will represent 70 percent of the budget deficit. We're moving into an era of permanent, huge budget deficits driven by the massive increases in spending and debt interest.

Government as
Big Daddy Employer

All this enormous spending flows through and into the hands of a giant federal work force. Officially the federal government, as of 2009, employs 2,774,000 people. But it's not quite as simple as that. That figure doesn't include uniformed military personnel. Adding them doubles the figure to 4.4 million. There are also 66,000 people who work in the legislative branch and for federal courts. Moreover, a lot of government's work is done by contractors or organizations that receive government grants. That means everyone from arms manufacturers to local charities, from Big Green environmental groups to individual researchers at universities. All these groups are only functioning because Congress has decided that some of our money would be better taken out of our pockets and put in theirs. Sometimes that is for a noble reason, sometimes it's in reward for campaign contributions, but in all cases there are people working only because they receive taxpayer money to do so.[10] They should really be counted as part of the federal government, too.

Of course, the government doesn't want you to think so, which means we can't go to the Office of Personnel Management for data. Instead we need to go to Professor Paul Light of New York University, who has done some fine work estimating the size of these shadowy branches of government.[11] He points out that while there are many good reasons for the government to use contractors (should the government really be in the business of making dentures for veterans, like it did until the 1950s?), the use of contracts and grants also disguises the true size of government: "Not only does the federal government's largely hidden workforce of contractors and grantees encourage the public into believing that it truly can get more for less, it diffuses accountability."

Professor Light doesn't object to the size of government per se, but rather to its lack of accountability. Indeed, the very failure of the Office of Personnel Management to keep records of the number of quasi-governmental employees suggests to him that the government has something to hide: "Contractors and grantees do not keep count of their employees, in part because doing so would allow the federal government and scholars like me to estimate actual labor costs, and state and local governments make no effort whatsoever to quantify the number of hours their employees spend administering federal mandates."

Nevertheless, Professor Light, using the federal government's procurement database, estimated that in 1999 "the true size of the federal workforce was approximately 11 million, including 1.8 million civil servants, 870,000 postal workers, 1.4 million military personnel, 4.4 million contractors, and 2.5 million grantees." By 2005, only six years later, the true size of government had reached 14.6 million employees.

Even if government has just grown at the same rate as it did between 1999 and 2005—which is a conservative assumption given the massive stimulus spending, bailouts, and other spending increases under the Obama administration—that would mean another 4.7 million employees dependent on taxpayer funding since 2005, bringing the total true size of government to nearly 20 million employees. Once we add in state and local government employees, another 19.5 million people (local bureaucrats, teachers, firefighters, police officers, and so on),[12] we reach the astonishing conclusion that close to 40 million Americans are employed in some way on government business, which means about 26 percent of the American labor force owes its living to the taxpayer.[13] That's one in every four workers. Or to put it another way, it's about twice the number of people employed in mining, construction, and manufacturing; so we have twice as many bureaucrats and public "servants" as we do builders. Somehow that doesn't seem like the American way.

The One-Minute
Public Sector Manager

When I first joined the British government's Department of Transport fresh out of college, I had a wily old boss who had been a civil servant for thirty years. "Iain," he told me, "if you want to make a career of this, you have to remember one thing. Your success is measured in how big your staff and budget are."

By that measure, my boss was a great success; in three years at the Department of Transport he more than doubled his budget. I noted that intelligent managers who actually solved problems were, as my wily old boss predicted, routinely passed over for promotion in favor of those who found more problems requiring more staff.

In government, performance is judged by increases in funding. The cost-cutting boss is viewed with suspicion, even outright hostility, by his peers, as letting the side down. Academic research on how government bureaucracies function—the study of bureaucracy is a sub-field of what is known as "public choice theory"—has borne this out. But really the facts speak for themselves. As columnist and former White House staffer Jim Pinkerton has pointed out, in the nineteenth century, 50 percent of Americans lived on farms and the United States Department of Agriculture had 2,000 employees. Today, only 2.5 percent of Americans live on farms but the USDA has more than 100,000 employees.[14]

What is true for the bureaucracy is true for those who rely on government grants—they are judged by their ability to sustain federal funding for their projects. Take, for instance, Penn State climatologist Michael Mann. Dr. Mann was deeply implicated in the "climategate" scandal of November 2009, when emails leaked from a British university showed that some of the world's leading climatologists discussed how to manipulate data, suppress inconvenient studies that contradicted their work, and evade British freedom of information laws. A Penn State inquiry into Dr. Mann's conduct was forthright in how academic success is measured:

> The results achieved by Dr. Mann in the period 1999-2010, despite [...] stringent requirements, speak for themselves: He served as principal investigator or co-principal investigator on five NOAA[National Oceanic and Atmospheric Admin]-funded and four NSF[National Science Foundation]-funded research projects. During the same period, Dr. Mann also

served as co-investigator of five additional NSF- and NOAA-
funded research projects, as well as on projects funded by the
Department of Energy (DOE), the United States Agency for
International Development (USAID), and the Office of Naval
Research (ONR). This level of success in proposing research,
and obtaining funding to conduct it, clearly places Dr. Mann
among the most respected scientists in his field. Such success
would not have been possible had he not met or exceeded the
highest standards of his profession for proposing research.[15]

If academic success depends on achieving "the highest standards...for
proposing research" that wins federal funds, it is not hard to see how
government funding can corrupt honest, disinterested science.

The bureaucrat's money, of course, has to come from someone—and
that someone is you. Every time government takes it upon itself to regulate
something, to manage something, to set up a subsidy or a welfare
program, you're paying for it. Government tries to justify this by convinc-
ing you that what it does is essential or compassionate or good for us. But
the fact that government has grown to such monstrous proportions and
saddled us with unsustainable debt leads to the obvious conclusion that
much of what government does can't be necessary and is manifestly not
good for us; and as for compassion, isn't that a virtue more associated
with individual charity than red tape-spinning bureaucrats?

Unhappy Meals

Sometimes, even in a liberal setting, the political class can overreach.
Take for instance, Eric Mar, Supervisor for District 1, the Richmond
District, of the City and County of San Francisco Board of Supervisors.
Mr. Mar is very much an exemplar of the modern political class, and the
story of his career and his aims embodies many of the themes in this book.
Before becoming a full-time politico, he was an associate professor of
Asian-American and Ethnic Studies at San Francisco State University.

He was also assistant dean for New College Law School in San Francisco, where he taught a course on "critical race theory."

As well as being a lawyer-academic, Mar is also a community organizer. His website says: "As a longtime community leader, Eric has led neighborhood and citywide efforts to preserve and expand afford-able housing, to increase funding for parks and libraries, to improve services for youth and seniors, and to protect locally owned neighbor-hood businesses from unfair competition from big corporations like Starbucks."

His community leadership even extends to the radicalization of his students—on your dime at a state-supported school. He boasts, under the heading "Progressive Teacher, Progressive Attorney": "Since 1992, Eric has taught Asian American and Ethnic Studies at San Francisco State University where he has mentored and supported hundreds of young people to become active in their communities and the political process."

His other progressive credentials are impeccable, even including labor union activism:

> Eric is the past director of the Northern California Coalition for Immigrant Rights and a longtime social justice activist with the Chinese Progressive Association and other grassroots organizations. As a public interest attorney, he served on the Human Rights Committee of the State Bar of California and the Civil Rights Committee of the National Asian Pacific American Bar Association. He is an ally of the labor move-ment and a past shop steward with SEIU Local 790.[16]

Mar intended to run for the San Francisco Board of Supervisors in 2000, but his house burned down the day his daughter was born, leaving him without a qualifying residence. He stood instead for election to the Board of Education, where he gained a strong record of spending taxpayer money. He also proposed a mandatory district-wide school rally against the Iraq War in 2003. Superintendent Arlene Ackerman objected, and a compromise was reached whereby the Board voted for a district-wide public discussion about the possibility of war with Iraq.

During his time on the Board of Education, Mar and Ackerman engaged in a running battle over education policy. Mar reportedly told a Chinese-language newspaper that Ackerman's attitude to Chinese-Americans would be considered in her yearly performance appraisal. This sparked a furious reaction from another wing of the progressive community, with the president of the San Francisco Black Leadership Forum calling Mar's suggestion "unacceptable, irresponsible, [and] intolerable."[17]

Nevertheless, with this strong record of progressive policy behind him, Mar was elected to the Board of Supervisors in 2008. He reached national fame, though, with a proposal he sponsored in 2010 to ban restaurants from giving away toys with meals unless they were deemed nutritious, and included fruits and vegetables. The "Happy Meal Ban" was vetoed by San Francisco's mayor, Gavin Newsom, in a rare outbreak of common sense. Showing rather less common sense, the Council overrode the veto. Mar called the vote "crucial" in the battle against obesity. "It's a survival issue," he said.

Even Comedy Central's *The Daily Show with Jon Stewart*, generally a friend of "progressive" politics, found this proposal egregious. *Daily Show* "correspondent" Aasif Madvi asked Mar whether his daughter enjoyed Happy Meals. Mar replied that she did not, because she had learned lots about the fast food industry from watching Morgan Spurlock's shockumentary *Super Size Me* with him.

> **Mandvi:** "So she learned from her parents?"
> **Mar:** "That's a large part of it."
> **Mandvi:** (staring in wide-eyed disbelief) "Would it be hard to pass a law to force Netflix to send 'Super Size Me' to every parent in San Francisco?"
> **Mar:** "We can't force Netflix, a private company, to do something like that."

Mandvi: "Are you serious right now?"
Mar: "We have no power to force Netflix or a private company like that to change a business practice."
Mandvi: "So on one hand, you're like, 'We can't do that' but on the other hand, you are doing that."

Mar stumbled over his answer because he had no good answer to the common sense riposte of it being up to parents, not the government, to educate children about nutrition, and up to parents, not the government, to make food choices for their family.

Mar is a great example of today's elected local politician. His entire career has been lived on the public payroll, in higher education or government office, and he has devoted his life to politicizing everything he can get his hands on. What makes him particularly noteworthy, however, is that he has made it his legitimate role to steal candy from babies. That is government in a nutshell: it clips money from your wallet, tries to regulate your every decision, and might even snatch that Happy Meal from your child's hands; and while it tries to justify what it does in the name of protecting the public, what the bureaucracy is really doing is stealing you blind.

PART TWO

STAND AND DELIVER!

CHAPTER THREE

THE TAX ARMY

In 1998, the owner of a Texas oil firm testified that sixty-four IRS agents—two for each of his employees—broke down the doors to his offices and announced, "IRS! This business is under criminal investigation. Remove your hands from the keyboard and back away from the computers!"

The taxman these days is less an officious bean counter and more like a cop from a stereotypical banana republic. To call it an "army" of tax collectors is pretty accurate, because not only are there more of them than officers in the real army, but a good proportion of them are armed.

There's also an extraordinary deference shown to the IRS by the courts. The IRS wins something like 90 percent of its cases, a record that would be the envy of any law firm, or any other government agency for that matter. Yet the IRS comes with a litany of abuse in its wake. There are examples of Fourth Amendment breaches, denial of jury trials, and no-knock raids that would have the Left screaming with outrage if they were done to catch terrorists; as it is all done in the name of keeping the federal government going, though, not a whimper of dissent reaches the pages of Daily Kos.

On February 2, 2010, the following notice appeared on FedBizOps. org, the federal government's version of Craigslist:

> The Internal Revenue Service (IRS) intends to purchase sixty Remington Model 870 Police RAMAC #24587 12 gauge pump-action shotguns for the Criminal Investigation Division. The Remington parkerized shotguns, with fourteen inch barrel, modified choke, Wilson Combat Ghost Ring rear sight and XS4 Contour Bead front sight, Knoxx Reduced Recoil Adjustable Stock, and Speedfeed ribbed black forend, are designated as the only shotguns authorized for IRS duty based on compatibility with IRS existing shotgun inventory, certified armorer and combat training and protocol, maintenance, and parts.
>
> Submit quotes including 11% Firearms and Ammunition Excise Tax (FAET) and shipping to Washington DC.

These are serious pieces of hardware. As a character once said on the British comedy series *Yes Minister*, "Perhaps the government thinks that a tax is the best form of defense."

Why does the IRS need such serious artillery? Well, it all goes back to prohibition, when the IRS began to think of itself as a law enforcement agency, an attitude enshrined in the story of it bringing down Al Capone. There's even a special section on the IRS website about the Capone investigation,[1] which they say is being made available despite the confidentiality of federal tax records. According to Jonathan Eig, author of *Get Capone*, the IRS actually railroaded Al Capone in a sham trial. He was sentenced to eleven years in prison on five charges of tax evasion; previously, no one had served more than two or three years for the same offenses. Nevertheless, this great triumph cemented the IRS opinion of itself as a law enforcement body, something that was confirmed after the end of prohibition when the IRS was given power to collect taxes and duties on guns with the passage of the National Firearms Act in 1934. This law effectively banned "gangster" weapons on the grounds that they were not compatible with "militia" use under the Second Amendment. In effect, the IRS had become the prime agent of gun control in America.

Today, the IRS has 2,700 special agents who are sworn law-enforcement officers. About one in five revenue agents—that's the people you meet with face to face as opposed to the backroom staff—are armed agents. That tells you a lot about the psychology of the IRS. And the IRS is big.

The IRS has 106,000 employees and a budget of $12 billion. The average IRS employee earns $48,100, which compares favorably to the average male income of $33,161 and even more favorably to the average female income of $20,867.[2] An average tax examiner (a bean counter) earns $42,035; a tax specialist (a senior bean counter) earns $63,547; and an internal revenue agent (a top bean counter and sometimes an armed bean counter) earns $91,507...all paid, of course, by the taxes they collect. IRS bean counters, armed or otherwise, also get a fine selection of benefits at our expense: "Tax-deferred retirement savings and investment plans with employer matching contributions, health insurance, and life insurance."[3]

The IRS collects more than $2 trillion in tax dollars out of our pockets, at a cost of about 50 cents per 100 dollars collected. But that's not the only cost the IRS and its local equivalents impose on our economy.

The Cost of Compliance

The Tax Foundation, the country's oldest think tank, concluded in their last comprehensive report (in 2006) that complying with IRS rules—everything from tax planning and preparation to defending yourself in audits—costs our economy about $265 billion a year.[4] (In 1990, the figure was $108 billion in inflation-adjusted dollars. The Tax Foundation estimated that the costs of compliance, adjusted for inflation, would reach $338 billion in 2010 and $406 billion by 2015.) In terms of time lost, 6 billion hours, it's the equivalent to a workforce of almost 3 million people doing nothing else but dealing with the IRS.

All this time and money is the result of the tax code's becoming increasingly complex. In 1954, there were 409,000 words dedicated to the Internal Revenue Code, 172,000 concerning the income tax. Today the code numbers more than 2.1 million words, with 1.3 million dedicated to the income tax. That's only half the story, though (actually, far less than half). The greater part of the federal tax system is regulations covering how the code is administered. From 1955 to 2005, the number of words dedicated to tax regulation had jumped from about a million to more than 7 million. Who benefits from a complex tax code? Well, tax accountants, of course, but also government employees, because all these regulations have to be digested and enforced by an army of bureaucrats—your tax dollars at work, taxing you.

And those bureaucrats aren't above acting like Al Capone themselves. Before the passage of the Taxpayers' Bill of Rights in 1998, stories abounded of out-of-control district directors making taxpayers' lives a misery, destroying their livelihoods and in some tragic cases driving them to suicide. Even today, however, IRS employees have been charged with making false statements, soliciting bribes, and practicing extortion, not to mention identity theft.

A report by the Treasury Inspector General for Tax Administration in 2007 found that hundreds of IRS computers had been stolen (at least 490 in a three-year period), that employees were not properly encrypting data, and that control of access to passwords was lax. This meant that the tax affairs and personal data of a "significant number" of taxpayers were open to identity theft or worse. In many cases, however, it was the IRS officials who were prying where they shouldn't and in some cases were engaging in identity theft themselves.

Of course, the underlying reason why identity theft and similar crimes are possible at the IRS is because the Tax Code is so complicated. It requires us to submit a massive amount of financial detail to back up our claims, which in turn is money for the identity thief. The IRS has access to mortgage details, credit card data, phone records, and even personal correspondence, to say nothing of banking and other financial records. If the Tax Code were far simpler—a fair flat tax or even a consumption-based tax, none of this would be available to the thieves.

Bill of Rights?
What Bill of Rights?

The fact that the IRS has the power to require us to provide all this information is just one of the ways in which the IRS operates as if the Bill of Rights didn't exist. According to Chris Edwards of the Cato Institute, the IRS has powers that turn our Constitution upside down.[5] For instance, the Fifth Amendment says that no one shall be deprived of liberty or property "without due process of law." This requirement, however, is frequently ignored by the IRS, which engages in summary judgments, enforcing them—depriving people of property—before the courts have been involved. Moreover, an essential part of due process is that the burden of proof should lie with the accuser. Yet in non-criminal tax cases, the burden of proof lies with the accused. As Edwards says, "Except in some narrow circumstances, the IRS does not have to prove the correctness of its determinations. When the IRS makes erroneous assessments, as it often does, citizens carry the burden to prove that they are wrong."

The IRS also voids the right of the accused to trial by jury because the U.S. Tax Court is defined as an administrative court, rather than a court governed by Article III of the Constitution, which means that no jury trial is required. The only way to get a jury trial for a civil tax case is by filing suit in a U.S. District Court *after* you have paid the alleged tax, penalties, and interest in full. So if you can't pay, the courts can't protect you, which means that a lowly peasant in King John's England in 1215, protected by the Magna Carta and its guarantee of a trial by jury, had more rights than you do against the IRS.

Then there's the Fourth Amendment, which protects us from "unreasonable searches and seizures" of our "persons, houses, papers and effects" and says that warrants for searches and seizures must have "reasonable cause." However, Section 7602 of the Tax Code gives the IRS power to ignore all that "for the purpose of ascertaining the correctness of any return," not on probable cause that you have defrauded the IRS. The information revolution has also made it easier for the IRS to search bank records and so on without you knowing.

Finally, there's a Fifth Amendment protection (that every moviegoer knows about) against self-incrimination. However, filing a tax return constitutes a waiver of that protection. The IRS can and does release your information to federal, state, and local authorities for both tax *and non-tax* law enforcement purposes. So, for some people, filing a tax return opens them up to the self-incrimination that the Fifth Amendment was supposed to protect them from. Yet the alternative to filing is not filing, which opens them up to prosecution for failure to file.

An astonishing example of how the IRS uses these privileges arose in the case of Charlie Engle, one of the few people to go to jail over the subprime crisis. Yet Engle was not a banker, knowingly taking massive risks with other people's property, but a mortgage borrower. He ended up in jail because one IRS agent took an interest in him, and used every power at his disposal to nail him, all without any probable cause.[6]

The IRS agent, Robert Nordlander, became interested in Charlie Engle after seeing a movie that Engle featured in, about ultra-marathon athletes running across the Sahara Desert. "Being the special agent that I am, I was wondering, how does a guy train for this because most people have to work from nine to five and it's very difficult to train for this part-time," Nordlander told Engle's grand jury. Nordlander admitted to the grand jury that when he sees someone driving a Ferrari, he will check to see if that person had reported enough money to pay for it. The *New York Times*' Joe Nocera raised an eyebrow at this: "When I called Mr. Nordlander and others at the I.R.S. to ask whether this was an appropriate way to choose subjects for criminal tax investigations, my questions were met with a stone wall of silence."

It turned out that Mr. Engle did indeed make enough money to indulge in his hobby, but he had a low taxable income because of a tax write-off against a business loss. Despite this, Agent Nordlander remained convinced that Engle was hiding income, and continued investigations; he put Mr. Engle under surveillance, engaged in "dumpster diving," and even indulged his inner James Bond, sending an attractive female agent to trap Engle into an indiscretion.

This agent, Ellen Burrows, did indeed secure an indiscretion from Engle, but it had nothing to do with his tax affairs. While Burrows was wearing a wire, Engle confessed that his mortgage broker had submitted inflated "stated income" when Engle applied for two "liar loans," the type of subprime loan where an applicant did not submit supporting documentation confirming his or her income.

Joe Nocera sums up the weakness of the case against Mr. Engle: "[T]he more I looked into it, the more I came to believe that the case against him was seriously weak. No tax charges were ever brought, even though that was Mr. Nordlander's original rationale. Money laundering, the suspicion of which was needed to justify the undercover sting, was a nonissue as well. As for that 'confession' to Ms. Burrows, take a closer look. It really isn't a confession at all. Mr. Engle is confessing to his mortgage broker's sins, not his own."

In the ensuing case for mortgage fraud, the prosecutors persuaded the mortgage broker to testify against Mr. Engle. The broker concerned was also prosecuted, but received a reduced sentence—less than Engle's—because of his willingness to testify against him.

Now Charlie Engle may well have committed a crime, and so he should be punished. The fact is, however, that virtually all the investigations against him were based on a flimsy hunch by an IRS agent. That's exactly the sort of arbitrary government the Bill of Rights is supposed to protect us against.

Meanwhile, the mega-corporation General Electric employs 975 tax specialists and, despite making domestic profits of $5 billion in 2010, has no tax liability for the year.[7] GE supremo Jeffrey Immelt is chairman of President Obama's Council on Jobs and Competitiveness.

Listen to the Advocate

One of the things the Taxpayers' Bill of Rights did was set up an advocate for the rest of us within the IRS. Every year, the National Taxpayer Advocate reports to Congress about the most serious problems faced by taxpayers when dealing with the IRS. Occasionally, Congress listens.

In 2010 the Advocate, Nina E. Olson, reported to Congress that the single most significant problem facing the taxpayer was the size and complexity of the Internal Revenue Code. As she put it, "No-one wants to feel like a 'tax chump'—paying more while suspecting that others are taking advantage of loopholes to pay less. Because of tax complexity, taxpayers often suspect that the 'special interests' are receiving tax breaks while they themselves are paying full freight." She's right, and her proposed solution is correct too: "Everything must be put on the table, and we must understand that, in exchange for lower rates, some tax breaks will be eliminated immediately and others will be phased out. If tax reform proceeds on a revenue-neutral basis, however, the average taxpayer's liability will not change, and we will end up with a tax system that is simpler, more transparent, and easier and cheaper for taxpayers to navigate."

You can almost hear the cries of horror emanating from the IRS. A simpler, more efficient tax code will mean fewer IRS agents, fewer audits, and fewer prosecutions. The very concept strikes at the heart of how the IRS sees itself.

Ms. Olson has a lot of other observations as well: the IRS is being asked to act as a provider of social benefits; it receives disproportionate reward for its enforcement activities; its Wage & Investment Division is distracted by keeping phone systems and web sites up rather than dealing with taxpayer inquiries; and many others.

Most serious, however, is the fact that it is still the case that the IRS doesn't regard a taxpayer's other debt as an "allowable expense" when computing how much a taxpayer can reasonably pay when he or she needs to settle a debt with the IRS. So if you have a credit card debt, a court-ordered payment like alimony or child support, a student loan or a medical bill, the IRS doesn't take those payments into account. You have to pay the IRS any money that would normally go to these creditors. Ms. Olson cites a survey that found that half of a group of delinquent taxpayers who were forced into bankruptcy were deemed able to pay based on the IRS analysis standards.

Of course, this causes the victimized taxpayer even more problems, which often result in further tax delinquency. The same study found that 74 percent of taxpayers who were subject to IRS collection procedures had "one or more subsequent tax delinquencies or unfiled returns, even though they had no outstanding assessed tax liabilities before the period under study." It becomes a vicious cycle of debt and tax problems, although from the IRS's point of view, it's just more business.

A related problem the Advocate identified is that IRS collection policies channel taxpayers into installment agreements they cannot afford. If you owe the IRS less than $25,000 and agree to pay in full within five years, the IRS has a "streamlined" installment agreement that you can qualify for that means you don't have to have IRS agents crawling all over your personal finances. However, an IRS study found that more than a quarter of taxpayers requesting streamlined payment plans could not afford them. Ms. Olson also found that the IRS sometimes places taxpayers into these streamlined plans without their consent— "a practice that may violate the law," she points out. This sends many people into the same vicious cycle of non-payment we've just discussed.

Altogether, the National Taxpayer Advocate detailed twenty-one significant problems for taxpayers based on IRS practices in her 2010 report. She also identified four areas of past concern that the IRS had not addressed adequately. It is no wonder that her first recommendation to Congress was "Enact tax reform now."

Perhaps the Founders knew what they were doing in the Constitution when they didn't grant the federal government explicit authority to levy an income tax. That power didn't come until the Sixteenth Amendment, passed in 1913—and we've been paying the price ever since. If the bureaucrats have their way, the shakedown will get even worse.

Preparing Taxes without a License

The first thing the IRS wants to do is to make it more difficult for you to file your taxes. Most people who have slightly complex tax affairs use a third party to prepare their tax forms. These businesses are usually small scale, often part-time or just operating around tax season, with few formal qualifications bar a great deal of experience in filling out tax forms. That isn't good enough for the IRS. They want third party tax preparers to go through a formal licensing procedure, a proposal that would adversely affect 700,000 tax preparers and 87 million taxpayers, according to the Institute for Justice (IJ). Licensing would inevitably drive up the cost of tax preparation and limit its suppliers to large companies that are able to absorb the cost of licensing.

This proposal would effectively force millions of taxpayers to forego the use of expert tax preparers, sending them towards pen-and-papers forms and incomprehensible tax guides, or to the IRS's own tax preparation software, available for free at the IRS web site (and why use commercial software costing up to $60 when you can use free software?).

Indeed, the IRS has been "working with" commercial software companies to force them to use the IRS site. Yet, as IRS Representative Dee Stepter told WDAM News in Missouri, "Now a lot of these software companies also provide free electronic filing through their own website, but to access free file, you have to go through irs.gov. It doesn't mean that they aren't reputable, but if you want to go to free file, go through the free file alliance you must go through irs.gov."[8] It should also be noted that the IRS software does not give you any guidance—if you miss an important deduction using it, tough luck.

It's interesting also that the proposed regulations contain an exemption for CPAs and lawyers, even if those professions have never looked at a tax form in their life. The IJ's Dan Alban, himself a lawyer, called shenanigans on the IRS in an article in the Daily Caller, explaining just why the IRS was probably pushing the rule. First, he noted that license costs would create a barrier to entry into the market, benefiting large corporations (H&R Block initially supported the requirement). More importantly, however:

> [M]andatory licensure gives the IRS substantially more control over tax return preparers. In fact, it makes preparers actually dependent on the IRS for their livelihood. That's a troubling new power dynamic that could give the IRS increased leverage in disputes such as disagreements with preparers over interpretations of the tax code. And it seems likely to endanger the role that a tax return preparer has as an advocate of his or her client—will preparers really be able to fully represent their clients' best interests in a dispute with the IRS when concerned about the possibility of having their license revoked?[9]

It is likely that the desired end result of the IRS is that the IRS does your taxes for you. That's not a prospect anyone should regard as acceptable. Yet that's not the worst the IRS has planned for you.

New Powers, New Forms, New Mistakes, New Lawsuits

Through Obamacare, the Obama administration tried to sneak through the greatest expansion in the IRS's powers in decades. As *CNN Money* reported:

> An all-but-overlooked provision of the health reform law is threatening to swamp U.S. businesses with a flood of new tax paperwork.

Section 9006 of the health care bill—just a few lines buried in the 2,409-page document—mandates that beginning in 2012 all companies will have to issue 1099 tax forms not just to contract workers but to any individual or corporation from which they buy more than $600 in goods or services in a tax year.

The stealth change radically alters the nature of 1099s and means businesses will have to issue millions of new tax documents each year.[10]

Few people currently get 1099s for "miscellaneous income." I get them for my freelance writing work and attach them religiously to my tax returns. But, as *The Wall Street Journal* explained:

> Under the new rules, if a freelance designer buys a new iMac from the Apple Store, they'll have to send Apple a 1099. A laundromat that buys soap each week from a local distributor will have to send the supplier a 1099 at the end of the year tallying up their purchases.
>
> The bill makes two key changes to how 1099s are used. First, it expands their scope by using them to track payments not only for services but also for tangible goods. Plus, it requires that 1099s be issued not just to individuals, but also to corporations.
>
> Taken together, the two seemingly small changes will require millions of additional forms to be sent out.
>
> "It's a pretty heavy administrative burden," particularly for small businesses without large in-house accounting staffs, says Bill Rys, tax counsel for the National Federation of Independent Businesses.

The purpose of the clause was to make tax write-offs more difficult and to vacuum up more tax dollars to help pay the appalling cost of Obamacare.

But that's not the only cost. As the *Wall Street Journal* points out:

> The notion of mailing a tax form to Costco or Staples each
> year to document purchases may seem absurd to small busi-
> ness owners, but that's not the worst of it, tax experts say.
>
> Marianne Couch, a principal with the Cokala Tax Group
> in Michigan and former chair of a citizen advisory group to
> the IRS on small business and self-employed tax issues, thinks
> the bigger headache will be data collection: gathering names
> and taxpayer identification numbers for every payee and
> vendor that you do business with.

The mind boggles as to how much time a freelancer would have to devote
to this activity. The *Wall Street Journal* had a great example: "Think
about a midsized trucking company. The back office would have to
collect hundreds of thousands of receipts from every gas station where
its drivers filled up and figure out where it spent more than $600 that
year. Then it would also need to match those payments to the stations'
corporate parents."[11]

Yet that's just the beginning. Millions more forms filed means at
least thousands of new mistakes made in submitting tax returns. That
means thousands more penalties applied and audits run. The IRS would
be clambering over small businesses like Santa Anna's troops storming
the Alamo.

Enough people complained that Senator Ben Nelson of Florida
offered an amendment in September 2010 to restrict the effect to firms
employing more than twenty-five people and spending more than $5,000
with one supplier, but the Senate rejected the amendment.

After the 2010 elections, however, the new Senate repealed the entire
provision by a vote of 83 to 17. As the *Wall Street Journal* reported,
"Democrats now claim that the infamous 1099 business reporting man-
date that the Senate repealed this week was an accident, as if they were
as surprised as everyone else to learn that this destructive provision had

crept by itself into law." [12] Congress experienced a rare outbreak of sense on this issue, and went on to repeal the provision.

The fact is, however, that the 1099 provision was symptomatic of the government's attitude that people are tax cheats and the IRS needs new powers to seize money that is rightfully the government's:

> During the Bush years, Democrats and more than a few Republicans convinced themselves that businesses were cheating the government out of revenues through deliberate under-reporting and various tax shelters.
>
> This notion prevailed at the Senate Finance Committee under both Democratic Chairman Max Baucus and Republican Chairman Chuck Grassley. Budget Chairman Kent Conrad was another evangelist. In its first budget, the Obama White House promised "robust" tax compliance enforcement "to narrow the annual tax gap of over $300 billion," in contrast to the lethargy of its predecessor.
>
> The 1099 ObamaCare footnote thus received no scrutiny at first because it was so mundane. Everyone in Washington agreed that corporations were stealing billions of dollars every year that rightfully belonged to Congress to spend....
>
> In the same Washington mindset, the 1099 mandate doesn't impose any more of a reporting burden than a European-style value-added tax.

Politicians always need to be reminded that tax money is not theirs—it's ours.

CHAPTER FOUR

RED TAPE
BONDAGE GAMES

In World War II, the Office of Strategic Services issued a document to its agents entitled *Simple Sabotage Field Manual,* suggesting how best to sabotage enemy production. In addition to the classic spy stuff like starting fires, the manual contains suggestions for slowing down company procedures. In short, they advise the use of bureaucracy as a method of sabotage. Here are a few of the tips they give for those infiltrating enemy production:

(1) Insist on doing everything through "channels." Never permit short-cuts to be taken in order to expedite decisions....

(3) When possible, refer all matters to committees, for "further study and consideration." Attempt to make the committees as large as possible—never less than five.

(4) Bring up irrelevant issues as frequently as possible.

(5) Haggle over precise wordings of communications, minutes, resolutions.

(6) Refer back to matters decided upon at the last meeting and attempt to re-open the question of the advisability of that decision.

(7) Advocate "caution." Be "reasonable" and urge your fellow-conferees to be "reasonable" and avoid haste which might result in embarrassments or difficulties later on.

(8) Be worried about the propriety of any decision—raise the question of whether such action as is contemplated lies within the jurisdiction of the group or whether it might conflict with the policy of some higher echelon.[1]

Other suggestions include:

(b) Managers and Supervisors

(1) Demand written orders....

(7) Insist on perfect work in relatively unimportant products; send back for refinishing those which have the least flaw....

(10) To lower morale and with it, production, be pleasant to inefficient workers; give them undeserved promotions. Discriminate against efficient workers; complain unjustly about their work.

(11) Hold conferences when there is more critical work to be done.

(12) Multiply paper work in plausible ways. Start duplicate files.

(13) Multiply the procedures and clearances involved in issuing instructions, pay checks, and so on. See that three people have to approve everything where one would do.

(14) Apply all regulations to the last letter.

Any rational student of American government would have to conclude, on the basis of this manual, that America was infiltrated by foreign agents some time ago, and they have been very successful in their work.

Ten Thousand Commandments

Every government office has some form of rule or regulation it enforces, ultimately at the point of a gun. In fact, when we joke that there are Ten Thousand Commandments out there, we're waaay understating the case.

Since 1995, the federal government has issued more than 60,000 regulations, all with the force of law. The ancient Athenians thought that it was important that all citizens understood the law that applied to them, so they inscribed it on bronze tablets available for all to see. By contrast, the Federal Register—our equivalent of those tablets—runs to some 60,000–70,000 pages each year. Good luck not falling afoul of those at some point.

Even President Barack Obama seems to recognize, or to recognize the importance of appearing to recognize, that the American economy is over-regulated. On January 18, 2010, he wrote an op-ed for the *Wall Street Journal* where he said:

> We're…getting rid of absurd and unnecessary paperwork requirements that waste time and money. We're looking at the system as a whole to make sure we avoid excessive, inconsistent and redundant regulation. And finally, today I am directing federal agencies to do more to account for—and reduce—the burdens regulations may place on small businesses. Small firms drive growth and create most new jobs in this country. We need to make sure nothing stands in their way.[2]

Fine words, but the proof of the pudding is in the eating. As an example of the new way forward on regulation, he cited the new Environmental Protection Agency (EPA) standards on fuel economy, which he suggests is a tasty dessert:

> When I took office, the country faced years of litigation and
> confusion because of conflicting rules set by Congress, federal
> regulators and states. The EPA and the Department of Trans-
> portation worked with auto makers, labor unions, states like
> California, and environmental advocates this past spring to
> turn a tangle of rules into one aggressive new standard. It was
> a victory for car companies that wanted regulatory certainty;
> for consumers who will pay less at the pump; for our security,
> as we save 1.8 billion barrels of oil; and for the environment
> as we reduce pollution.

In fact, the new regulations are almost indigestible. No one in the auto
industry has any idea how to meet their requirements while still supply-
ing the sort of car Americans want to drive. One thing is certain—the
attempts to meet the standards will result in vehicles that are both much
more expensive and much smaller, meaning many more deaths on the
road.

Moreover, the "confusion" the president talks about arose from EPA
bureaucrats' desire to muscle in on territory formerly occupied by the
Department of Transportation. Fuel economy standards have always
been set by that department. But former Governor Arnold Schwarzenegger of California had a mighty bureaucracy of his own—the California
Air Resources Board (CARB)—which has a privileged position under
federal law. Because of the unique geography and meteorology of California, CARB has the power to apply for waivers under the Clean Air
Act to solve local problems. Governor Schwarzenegger asked for such
a waiver to allow CARB to design a greenhouse gas emissions program
that would impose fuel economy standards. President Bush's EPA administrator, Stephen Johnson, denied such a waiver, on the grounds that it
would create the confusion President Obama talks about. It was Obama's
new administrator, Lisa Jackson, who created the confusion by granting
California's waiver!

Once the waiver was granted, regulatory chaos was bound to ensue. As former Virginia governor and U.S. senator George Allen and my colleague Marlo Lewis explain:

> Consumer preferences differ from state to state, so the same automaker typically sells a different mix of vehicles in each state. Only by sheer improbable accident would the average fuel economy...of an automaker's vehicles delivered for sale in one state be identical to that in other state (*sic*). But under the initial CARB program, each automaker would have to achieve the same average fuel economy...in every state that adopted California's standards. If all 50 states adopt the California program, then each automaker would have to manage 50 separate fleets, reshuffling the mix in each state regardless of consumer preference. A more chaotic scheme would be hard to imagine.[3]

So in stepped the EPA to solve the problem it had created. It wrested power from the Transportation Department, despite having no legal basis for doing so, by linking fuel economy standards to greenhouse gas emissions. American automakers, already dependent on federal goodwill thanks to the auto bailouts of 2008, readily accepted the scheme as preferable to regulatory chaos. Yet nixing the rule and the California waiver would be far better for them.

As for consumers, there's a high cost to be paid for smaller, higher-miles-per-gallon vehicles. As Allen and Lewis explain: "Lighter vehicles have less mass to absorb collision forces. Smaller vehicles provide less space between the occupant and the point of collision. The National Academy of Sciences has estimated that CAFE [Corporate Average Fuel Economy standards] contributed to an additional 1,300 to 2,600 fatalities and 13,000 to 26,000 serious injuries in 1993 (a typical year)." This program is a true example of "death by regulation."

The Cost of
the Regulatory State

In 2005 the Small Business Administration published a study by Mark Crain of Lafayette College that provided a comprehensive estimate of regulatory costs. His conclusion was that complying with regulation cost the economy $1.1 trillion in 2004, when our GDP was $11 trillion.[4] Every year, my friend and colleague Wayne Crews updates these figures in his analytical report, *Ten Thousand Commandments: An Annual Snapshot of the Federal Regulatory State*. For 2010, he found that the cost of the regulatory state had grown to just under $1.7 trillion, outpacing the growth in GDP. That puts it in the same league as the current federal deficit. And it means that regulatory costs are likely to skyrocket as the federal budget does likewise.

Yet, regulation being the sort of creature it is, we could even expect an increase in regulation if the federal government retreated from its tax-and-spend course. Regulation is insidious. We don't notice it as readily as we notice increases in tax or direct spending, so it's an easy way to expand government on the sly, which is why bureaucrats love regulation. They get the results they want, and we pay for it.

The regulators' interests are not our interests. If Washington had really wanted to stimulate the economy, it could have slashed $150 billion worth of regulations on business—at no cost to the taxpayer. Instead, it rang up $150 billion in 2008 on your bill to pay companies (or state and local governments) to hire workers for projects that didn't need to be done.

To put the regulatory burden in perspective, in 2007, before the financial crisis hit, annual *pretax* corporate profits were $1.9 trillion. Regulatory costs to businesses ($1.1 trillion) were about 60 percent of their profits. Just a small amount of regulatory relief could have boosted profits by ten percent or more, meaning more jobs and higher wages. Then there's the cost of policing this regulatory state. The combined administrative cost of economic and environmental regulation amounts to $55 billion. That money is administered by 266,300 bureaucrats.

Aren't you glad they're there? Since 2000, the staffing figures have increased by 54 percent (11 percent if you exclude the new TSA employees; but even then costs rose by 30 percent).[5]

Strangled in Red Tape

That fact should also tell you something about one of the biggest lies told by liberals over the past few years: that the Bush years were some sort of deregulatory cascade, where rule after rule was rolled back, putting the public in more and more danger. Nothing could be further from the truth. The Bush years saw a massive bloating of the regulatory state, with more and more rules being issued by an out-of-control executive branch that didn't seem to care what its only elected member thought about it. To be sure, the Bush White House tried to reduce the rate of new regulation, but it certainly couldn't reduce the size and scope of the regulatory state.

We don't just have staffing numbers and budgets to back this up. We have the documentary evidence of the Federal Register itself, where new regulations are published every week, and also the Code of Federal Regulations (CFR), which is the regulatory equivalent of the Tax Code and its regulations. In 2007, to take a year at random from the Bush years, the Federal Register weighed in at 72,000 pages for the year (perhaps government lawyers get paid by the word?), while the CFR topped out at 145,816 pages—8,000 pages longer than it was in 2000.

Page counts don't tell you everything, though. The real indicator is the number of so-called "major rules" that have affects nearly every American, whether, for example, by increasing the cost of our automobiles, or by putting more burdens on our local education departments, or increasing the cost of our local taxes. The Bush administration brought in more than seventy new major regulations that increased burdens on Americans, compared with twenty-three that reduced them (the ones the Left complains about). Interestingly, the agencies that were not responsible to the White House's regulatory approval, like the Securities and

Exchange Commission and the Federal Communications Commission, were responsible for more than half of the deregulatory moves, so it's not as if the Bush administration can claim much credit (or blame, if you're on the Left) for them, either.

Admittedly, President Bush was much less of a regulator than President Clinton. The second term of the Clinton presidency saw major rules brought in at the rate of nineteen a year. A whole slew of "midnight regulations" at the end of the Clinton presidency pushed 2001's extra regulatory burden to more than $13 billion. President Bush didn't engage in any comparable push for "midnight regulations," but altogether the decade 2000 to 2009 saw 39,540 new final rules introduced, all of which have to be administered and enforced.

There's also the "Regulatory Plan and the Unified Agenda of Federal Regulatory and Deregulatory Actions," which appears in the Federal Register each December. It lists rules that have recently been completed together with those anticipated for the next twelve months by each of the sixty federal agencies that have rulemaking powers. It's therefore a great guide to how the regulatory pipeline is flowing. In 2010, the Agenda told us that agencies were working on 4,225 rules, all the way from "prerules" to just-completed regulations. Of these, the most—580—were promulgated by the Department of Treasury, followed by the Environmental Protection Agency at 345. Ten Thousand Commandments has an updated list every year, and you can get that from CEI's website at www.cei.org/10KC.

The Agenda also tells us what rules are "economically significant"— meaning that they'll have an impact on the nation of more than $100 million when implemented. There were 224 of these in 2009, so the cost to the nation will be at least $22 billion, but it could well be far more than that. The Agenda doesn't tell us how much the rule will cost, just whether it's over $100 million.

One thing we do know about the Agenda's rules is how many of them will significantly affect small businesses, thanks to the Regulatory Flexibility Act. The 2010 Agenda listed 845 such rules, more than 60 percent of them from just five agencies—the departments of Agriculture, Commerce, Health and Human Services, the Environmental Protection Agency, and the Federal Communications Commission.

We also know how many rules involve the Feds getting state and local governments to do their dirty work for them. The Unfunded Mandates Act, passed in 1995 to rein in this practice, requires such rules to be highlighted. In 2010, 547 rules will affect state governments and 346 will affect local governments.

The Anti-Stimulus

When you work out how much these rules cost businesses, you can see why small businesses always suffer the most. According to the best estimates, regulations costs small businesses (those with fewer than twenty workers) $10,585 per employee. For large firms (500 workers or more) the cost is $7,755 per employee. Indeed, regulation is a real barrier to a firm's growth. The National Federation of Independent Businesses (NFIB) has found that at some point between twenty and thirty-five employees, firms hire a dedicated regulatory professional.[6] However, as Andrew Langer of the Institute for Liberty noted, speaking before the United States Senate in 2010,

> Until those businesses reach that magic number, it is generally the small business owner, that owner's spouse, or some trusted employee within the business who is responsible for filtering out regulatory obligations and figuring out what needs to be done in order to be in compliance. Because these individuals do not have the prior regulatory experience or training, it takes far longer for them to become aware of their obligations under the law, and just what those obligations entail.

Some have contended that the regulatory burden has decreased with the advent of computers—but if it has, the effect is small. Here's Langer again:

Technology alone cannot solve the problem. More than filing forms and storing copies, paperwork requirements
involve understanding what the government wants and how
they want it, gathering the necessary information and organizing it properly, determining what to keep and for how
long, etc. Then there is the cost. Even with the most efficient
computer equipment, documentation is not cheap. People
must organize and input the necessary data, and people are
expensive.

The number of regulations that apply to small businesses is astounding.
Even businesses with one employee have to comply with no fewer than
ten costly regulations, including the Fair Labor Standards Act, Social
Security matching and deposits, Medicare, FICA, the Equal Pay Act, the
Occupational Safety and Health Act, and, of all things, the Polygraph
Protection Act. By the time you get to a hundred employees, the regula-
tions to be complied with will have more than doubled, each to be applied
to every employee.

   We should also recognize that people who spend their time filling in
forms aren't working for the business owner except in the most trivial
sense. They're working for the government in all but name. In some ways,
the many thousands of regulatory professionals should be added to our
estimate of government employees. Yet once again, the government
doesn't pay for their employment, the business owner does. Yet another
example of the government stealing you blind.

Political Entrepreneurs

   There are, of course, special interests backing the bureaucrats in just
about every case of regulation. But less well noted is the class of political
entrepreneurs who seek to gain from new regulations—sometimes just
by expanding the bureaucracy, sometimes more directly.

Sometimes a political entrepreneur uses the threat of regulation as a simple tool of extortion. University of Virginia politics professor Larry Sabato has pointed out how politicians who voted for a Bill that prevented the regulation of dentists under the Federal Trade Commission were rewarded by the American Medical Association and the American Dental Association. "[A] favorable vote was worth, on average, nearly $1,000 for a legislator's campaign kitty, and any cosponsor of the bill was in line for $1,800 more than went to House members who did not cosponsor the bill."[7]

Indeed, passing or opposing legislative or regulatory efforts has become a major source of income for politicians. Campaign contributions are often procured by a legislator's stance on a particular issue. Thus, one legislator may bang on about the need for regulation of an established industry, gaining him contributions from the established firms that can afford to pay for regulation and want to see upstart competitors priced out of the market. Once the regulation is established, the bureaucracy works to expand its frontiers—as ever, all at your expense.

What makes things really interesting is how the fattest of fat cat bureaucrats often move between the bureaucracy, regulated industry, and special interest groups. Take, for example, David Doniger, policy director of the Natural Resources Defense Council, and Cathy Zoi, who was until recently an Obama appointee at the Department of Energy. My friend Ron Arnold of the Center for Defense of Free Enterprise has done quite a bit of digging into their career paths, and the term "revolving door" seems appropriate.

David Doniger began working at the Natural Resources Defense Council (NRDC) in 1978. He lobbied hard for the Montreal Protocol (banning substances that affect the ozone layer) in 1987 and the Clean Air Act Amendments (which introduced substantial extra regulation) in 1990. In 1992 he went into the bureaucracy, becoming counsel to the head of the U.S. Environmental Protection Agency's clean air program, and after that, the agency's director of climate change policy.

Doniger spent another year at the White House Council on Environmental Policy, but then returned to NRDC as policy director for the group's climate center. As Ron says, "As part of his work with NRDC, Doniger heads a legal committee that litigates against rules he helped write while in government."

Cathy Zoi is an even more interesting case. Here's Zoi career path, as summarized by Ron Arnold:

> During the early years of the Clinton administration, Zoi was chief of staff in the White House Office on Environmental Policy in 1994 and 1995, then went over to EPA in 1995 where she pioneered the government's Energy Star program.
>
> Zoi spent some years working overseas, serving as assistant director general of the New South Wales EPA in Sydney, Australia, from 1996 to 1999. And she spent some time from 2003 to 2007 as group executive director at the Bayard Group (now Landis + Gyr Holdings), a world leader in energy measurement technologies and systems.
>
> In 2007, Zoi became chief executive officer of former Vice President Gore's Alliance for Climate Protection [ACP], remaining there until 2009 when she rejoined the federal government as an Obama appointee.

Zoi became Assistant Secretary for Energy Efficiency and Renewable Energy (which she clearly loves and has worked to promote) until October 2010, when she was promoted to be Acting Undersecretary for Energy, with responsibility for fossil fuels (which she clearly hates and has worked to destroy). She then left government to go work for George Soros on a "green energy" investment fund. Moreover:

> Zoi's husband, Robin Roy, is vice president of projects and policy for Serious Materials, a company specializing in energy efficient building materials.

The Zois own 120,000 shares in Serious Materials and, as an officer of the company, Roy receives options on an additional 2,500 shares every month and will continue to do so until October 2012.

The Zois own between $250,000 and $500,000 in "founders shares" and another $15,000 to $50,000 in ordinary shares in Landis + Gyr, which makes smart meters, the advanced devices that enable real-time energy usage monitoring for greater efficiency and responsiveness by utilities and other price-setting agencies.

Remember that Robin Roy's wife was head of the Department of Energy section overseeing energy efficiency. This situation looked so shady that my colleague Chris Horner put in a request under the Freedom of Information Act for details on any discussions relating to Zoi's reported recusal on matters involving her husband's company. Chris picks up the story in October 2010:

The Department of Energy is now actively stonewalling the release of Zoi's records, subject to an appeal I filed last week. It seems that despite DoE claims that Zoi recused herself from her numerous conflicts—including policies currently rewarding her husband's company—no record of such recusals appeared in the sparse documents I obtained from DoE's designated ethics officer, under the Ethics in Government Act of 1978.

I also have requested Zoi's records discussing Gore, his former group the ACP and its affiliates, Landis + Gyr, Spain (documents I obtained earlier show her involvement in the attempted smear of Spanish researchers who debunked Obama's "green economy" claims regarding Spain), and addressing FOIA. For nearly six months, DoE has refused to respond to my requests.[8]

Zoi also appears to have retained ownership of Serious Materials and Landis + Gyr stocks while in office, despite divesting herself of other, less familial, holdings.

To make matters more interesting, in November 2010 the scientific magazine *Nature*, by virtue of a separate FOIA request, discovered some "relaxed" attitudes to hiring within Mrs. Zoi's department:

> Emails by an official in the weatherization program suggest that person knowingly sought to bypass regular hiring procedure, initially by trying to hire an individual from New West Technologies [a wind power company that received $2 million of taxpayer money from the stimulus act] into an adjunct advisory position with the intent to later make them a permanent federal employee. Although initial attempts to hire in this way weren't successful, the same person was then approached about advertized positions, with the decision in one case being made even before a short-list of candidates had been drawn up. One official forwarded the ad to the preferred candidate saying "I'm pretty sure you saw this, but I think this is the role for you :) happy applying!"
>
> The IG found the behavior violated a number of laws intended to promote fair competition for federal jobs and to prevent revolving door and other corrupt hiring arrangements. It has referred the recruiting officials involved for possible prosecution.

Then, in December 2010, with Mrs. Zoi in line for possible confirmation hearings for the permanent position at the Department of Energy, her husband suddenly moved jobs—to the NRDC, no less, as the group's director of clean energy strategy.

As for Chris's FOIA request, he was forced to appeal when the DoE continued to ignore it. In late January 2010, his appeal was turned down on the grounds that appeals are only allowed when the Department has refused a request. As the DoE simply stonewalled it, he apparently had no grounds to appeal. The DoE noted that Chris was within his rights to go to court to obtain the information that DoE is legally obligated, but seemingly unwilling, to release to him. The bureaucrats can game the system because they designed it and run it. They know that the wheels of justice grind exceeding slowly and that stonewalling in government can work more often than not. Cathy Zoi's compensation for her final year as director of the Alliance for Climate Protection in 2008 was more than $330,000. As acting under secretary, she received $165,000. There may be a very good reason she held on to those stocks. And now of course she's cashing in on her government experience with the Soros energy investment fund.

Another example from the revolving door, this time from the world of finance, is that of Amy Friend, revealed to the world by Tim Carney, a crusading investigative journalist with the *Washington Examiner*.[9] As the chief counsel to the U.S. Senate banking committee in 2008, Ms. Friend was instrumental in the bailouts of both the mortgage industry, including Bank of America, and Wall Street. After shoring up these monolithic institutions at the expense of smaller firms that did not make their mistakes, she helped then Senator Chris Dodd, a Democrat from Connecticut, draft and pass a massive bill that regulates both large and small finance houses.

In January 2011, Ms. Friend became a managing director at Promontory Financial Group, which bills itself as the "premier global financial services consulting firm." The press release announcing her appointment said,

> Ms. Friend, who joins the firm today, will work with Promontory clients on a wide range of issues, including risk management, governance, and the regulatory implementation of the Dodd-Frank Wall Street Reform and Consumer Protection Act of 2010, which, at 2,300 pages, is one of the most complex and wide-ranging overhauls of the financial regulatory framework in decades.[10]

That's the Dodd-Frank bill she helped write and pass. As Tim Carney says, "It's an unseemly storyline, but not a rare one in Washington: Bail them out. Regulate them. Then go to work for them."

Friend is another great example of a poacher turned gamekeeper turned poacher. She began her career as a political staffer for two congressional Democrats, Chuck Schumer and Rosa DeLauro. She worked as Minority General Counsel of the House Banking, Finance, and Urban Affairs Committee (now the House Financial Services Committee) and as General Counsel on the Consumer Affairs and Coinage Subcommittee. She then moved into the bureaucracy, becoming Assistant Chief Counsel of the Office of the Comptroller of the Currency, where she stayed until Dodd hired her in 2008.

Now, at Promontory, she will advise clients and prepare regulatory filings for them. As Carney notes, policy people are very valuable to K Street special interest and lobbying firms because, in the words of one lobbyist, "she knows what's on page twenty-three-[bleep]ing-hundred of that bill." As Carney notes, Friend not only wrote the bill, she wrote her own meal-ticket.

This would be bad enough, but Carney documents some interesting personal financial dealings as well:

> Two weeks before a Dodd-sponsored bailout of Fannie Mae passed the Senate, Friend purchased debt in [it]. She invested tens of thousands of dollars in bonds from the Federal Home Loan Bank Board, including purchases in June, when Dodd was pushing a housing bailout. Her 2008 investments included bailout barons AIG, Freddie Mac, Bank of America (which bought subprime king and Dodd benefactor Countrywide that year), Wells Fargo, and mortgage insurer MGIC.

Such conduct would raise an eyebrow or two on Wall Street, but it appears to be fine on North Capitol Street. Senator Dodd defended Ms. Friend when questions were raised about this. Carney does not suggest that

Friend *deliberately* used her Senate position to maximize her future earning potential. In fact, he thinks there was nothing deliberate about it; it's just the way big government works; it "is a breeding ground for revolving-door lobbyists."

Indeed, and only root-and-branch deregulation can break the chain. Deregulation leads to fewer rules, which leads to fewer lobbyists. One of the simplest ways to get money out of politics is to deregulate the economy. It is ironic that so many on the Left who say they want fewer lobbyists actually support the regulatory state that leads to more lobbyists.

The Lawyer-Bureaucrat

The lawyer-bureaucrat is in a powerful position. He can grow intimately familiar with the rules he administers (and in many cases drafts), and can parlay that into an even higher salary as a regulatory lawyer or K Street consultant, paid to advise people about—or protect them from—the regulations they know so well. Perhaps more disturbing is the case of the trial lawyer turned bureaucrat. If bureaucrats and their political allies are today's robber barons, then trial lawyers are the barons' border reivers, always on the look-out for businesses to shake down for some new alleged offense. The trial lawyers are major contributors to regulatory-imposing politicians, who in turn come up with new laws and regulations to keep the trial lawyers happy.

Occasionally, someone closely associated with the trial lawyers will step over the divide and take a senior position in the bureaucracy, where he can further advance the interests of his profession. Take for instance, David Strickland, now the administrator of the National Highway Traffic Safety Administration (NHTSA). From 1996 to 2001, Mr. Strickland served as associate director of the Association of Trial Lawyers of America, the trial lawyers' lobbyist group. While there, he lobbied to stop federal regulations pre-empting state-level regulations on various transportation issues.

For the next eight years, he served on the staff of the U.S. Senate Committee on Commerce, Science, and Transportation. He was the lead staffer in the oversight of NHTSA, the Federal Trade Commission, and the Consumer Product Safety Commission. He also served as the lead Senate staffer responsible for the formulation of the Corporate Average Fuel Economy (CAFE) reforms, which will lead to significantly more expensive automobiles. Once again we see the iron triangle of lobby-draft-regulate in action.

Mr. Strickland was head of the NHTSA during the investigation of Toyota-manufactured cars that experienced sudden, unexplained acceleration leading to accidents. Literally hundreds of lawsuits were launched against Toyota, starting in 2009. One driver, James Sikes, told several different media outlets about his supposedly fruitless struggles to regain control of his vehicle.

Yet, as investigative journalist Mike Fumento discovered when he investigated the cases:

> …the tall tales don't add up. In a Forbes.com piece , I exposed that Prius horror story: Almost everything driver James Sikes claimed was absurd, contradictory and perhaps physically impossible….
>
> And the mass reports of sudden-acceleration incidents just don't add up. Measured by reports to the National Highway Safety Administration, these same Toyotas were actually safe just a few months ago. And overseas they still are. Why have they suddenly gone nuts? Or have they?
>
> For most of 2009, the NHTSA got about one Toyota sudden-acceleration complaint a day. Then the automaker issued its September warning to customers that floor mats could trap accelerators—and complaints suddenly jumped.
>
> In November, Toyota announced a recall to fix sticky accelerators—and complaints jumped again. And in February, federal regulators announced they were widening their probe

to examine Toyota electronics—whereupon complaints shot into outer space at more than 150 a day.

Clearly, the biggest cause of Toyota sudden-acceleration complaints is media coverage.[11]

Mike also discovered that Sikes was several hundred thousand dollars in debt.[12]

The federal government announced an investigation into the Toyota acceleration story—and then sat on the results. In July 2010, an NHTSA whistleblower alleged that the Department of Transportation was blocking the release of the inquiry, which absolved Toyota of any blame. According to a report in the *Wall Street Journal*,

> George Person, who retired July 3 after 27 years at the National Highway Traffic Safety Administration, said in an interview that the decision to not go public with the data for now was made over the objections of some officials at NHTSA.
>
> "The information was compiled. The report was finished and submitted," Mr. Person said. "When I asked why it hadn't been published, I was told that the secretary's office didn't want to release it," he added, referring to Transportation Secretary Ray LaHood.[13]

Strickland's agency, NHTSA, actually took the blame, rather than the Secretary. It told the *Journal* that it was still reviewing the data and the investigation was still ongoing. According to Mr. Person, however, the issue was cut and dried:

> Since March, the agency has examined 40 Toyota vehicles where unintended acceleration was cited as the cause of an accident, Mr. Person said. NHTSA determined 23 of the vehicles had accelerated suddenly, Mr. Person said.

In all 23, he added, the vehicles' electronic data recorders or black boxes showed the car's throttle was wide open and the brake was not depressed at the moment of impact, suggesting the drivers mistakenly stepped on the gas pedal instead of the brake, Mr. Person said.

"The agency has for too long ignored what I believe is the root cause of these unintended acceleration cases," he said. "It's driver error. It's pedal misapplication and that's what this data shows."

Driver error was clearly the cause, which is exactly what Mike Fumento discovered when he investigated the cases. That means that all those lawsuits and other actions taken against Toyota were moot. Not for Toyota, however. The company had issued a recall of 8.5 million vehicles, paid a fine of $16.4 million for failing to report safety problems, and suffered worldwide damage to its reputation.

Finally, in February 2010, the Department of Transportation released the investigation, confirming what everyone except the salivating trial lawyers had known for the best part of a year:

> The Transportation Department said Tuesday that electronic flaws were not to blame for reports of sudden, unintended acceleration. Since 2009, Toyota has recalled more than 12 million vehicles globally over safety problems. The government's new findings bolstered Toyota's contention that the company had directly dealt with the problems through its recalls and is making safety paramount in its lineup....
>
> Transportation officials, helped by NASA engineers, said the 10-month study of Toyota vehicles concluded the acceleration cases could have been caused by mechanical defects already covered by recalls and suggested in some cases drivers hit the gas when they intended to press the brakes.[14]

Yet this didn't deter the trial lawyers. The Associated Press found a representative willing to say that the study didn't matter:

> Steve Berman, an attorney for plaintiffs in a class-action lawsuit against Toyota, said the report's findings were "in stark contrast to what Toyota drivers across the country experienced—and continue to experience—even after the series of recalls." He said there were too many reports of unwanted acceleration in vehicles fixed under the recall to eliminate electronics.

The question remains, however, to what extent did David Strickland influence what appears to be an unreasonable delay in the release of the report. As the Cato Institute's Walter Olson says, "Did it make a difference that the federal government has taken a proprietor's interest in major Toyota competitors GM and Chrysler, or that a former trial lawyer lobbyist heads the National Highway Traffic Safety Administration? Those questions might be worth a hearing at the newly reconstituted House Energy and Commerce Committee."

CHAPTER FIVE

IT'S FOR THE CHILDREN!

The government robber barons justify themselves by telling you that big government is for your own good; or, even better, "It's for the children!" What they really do is treat you like a child. The robber barons' regime is predicated on the idea that a bureaucrat knows better than a private individual what choices should be made; and in the process, big government infantilizes the people it "serves" or, more accurately, fleeces.

The Department of School Lunch Safety

Sometimes it literally is "for the children," and the children aren't very happy about it. Take, for example, the school district of St. Paul, Minnesota, which decided its job was to change students' dietary habits. In 2010, it declared that its schools would become "sweet-free zones." No longer would children be rewarded with candy. Cupcakes as birthday treats became a thing of the past. Brownies at bake sales were right out.

The reason given for the move was childhood obesity. School Super-intendent Valeria Silva discovered that the obesity rate in St. Paul's public schools was 40 percent, 11 percent above the national average. So she decided it was her job to do something about it by banning sweets— though there is very little evidence that such programs have any effect on obesity. The students realize this. "All my friends say, 'This really sucks,'" Misky Salad, a 10-year-old fifth-grader at Chelsea Heights Elementary told the *Star Tribune*. "A lot of us feel it should be up to us to determine what we should do with our bodies."[1] How very liberty-loving of her— but how utterly opposed to the nanny state. Perhaps the St. Paul public school teachers could better use their time expanding Misky's vocabulary beyond "sucks" rather than policing the possibility of her having cookies in her lunch bag.

Programs like St Paul's very rarely work because there is a wealth of sweet carbohydrates beyond the school gates. Take, for instance, Jamie's School Dinners, a project of British celebrity chef Jamie Oliver. Disgusted at the standard of food served in British schools, in 2004–2005 he started a project to bring healthier school lunches to the students. After a well-publicized TV series and no end of hectoring of children, lunch ladies, and politicians, the British government earmarked almost $1 bil-lion in public funds to improve the standard of school lunches, based on Oliver's advice.

It failed. Badly. Before *Naked Chef* Jamie's intervention, about 45 percent of students took school lunches. Five years later, after the govern-ment had spent vast amounts of money following Oliver's ideas about what makes a good school meal, that figure had slumped to 39 percent. Oliver might have made more nutritious meals, but they were favored by well-educated families, not the working-class families he had crusaded to save; they simply opted out of the program. Oliver brought his busy-body philosophy to Huntington, West Virginia in 2009–2010, with similar results. As the leftist website AlterNet reported, Oliver's meals exceeded the county's fat content and calories guidelines and were much more expensive:

> The reality behind "Food Revolution" is that after the first two months of the new meals, children were overwhelmingly unhappy with the food, milk consumption plummeted and many students dropped out of the school lunch program, which one school official called "staggering." On top of that food costs were way over budget, the school district was saddled with other unmanageable expenses, and Jamie's failure to meet nutritional guidelines had school officials worried they would lose federal funding and the state department of education would intervene.[2]

In England and Huntington, West Virginia, school administrators would have been better off remembering the adage that you can lead a horse to water but you can't make him drink. The real beneficiaries of such programs are not the children, who don't want them, but the bureaucrats who are employed to check the schools' progress, tabulate and file results, produce "performance indicators," issue reports, and, most important, demand more funding. It is programs like these that drive up education costs and continue to be funded when teaching budgets are cut. Bureaucrats always look after their own—their interests aren't yours.

Fahrenheit 451

Among their interests are book-burning—and driving small toymakers out of business—in the interest of a massive bureaucracy that is ostensibly protecting your children from lead consumption. The great political entrepreneur Henry Waxman, a Democrat congressman from California, led the charge for the Consumer Product Safety Improvement

Act (CPSIA), which tasks the Consumer Product Safety Council (CPSC) with checking all children's products for lead content, almost doubling that agency's budget in the process, from $80 million to $136 million by 2014 (just think how many extra bureaucrats that would pay for). The bill was supposed to protect children from bad products imported from China, but it was so sweepingly written, and its standards and penalties so onerous, that Mattel, the company behind six of the product recalls that presaged the law, quickly lobbied for and won an exception to the testing requirements. Mom and pop companies and libraries weren't so lucky. Dallas entrepreneur Phebe Phillips saw her successful business making plush toy animals collapse because the "new law raises the testing price for each product and in some cases, doubles or triples the costs. For some small companies, it can cost one year of total revenue just to meet the requirements of this law." [3]

Randy Hertzler, who imports toys from Europe, saw his business boom at first, as European toys were considered safer than Chinese-made ones. But *USA Today* reported, "He can't afford to do the testing that larger chains can.... 'Now Mattel is testing and making toys without any trouble at all, and those of us who were never the problem are in danger of losing our businesses,' says Hertzler, who runs EuroSource, based in Lancaster, Pa., with his wife and two sons." [4]

This point is crucial—what was killing these businesses was not that they were producing or selling lead-laden toys, but the crippling costs of merely complying with the regulations. The result has been a bonfire of toys and educational products. For instance, the American Educational Products company, which, as reported by the Alliance for Children's Product Safety, sells "teaching aids like flash cards, animal models, globes and relief maps" and has a "sterling safety record" is buckling under the weight of the regulations. As company president Michael Warring explained, "My 64 employees and I are finding it virtually impossible to manage the scale of this CPSIA-mandated testing....24 of my 64 employees would need to work full-time, year-round just to ensure compliance with CPSIA—even though our supply chain controls effectively manage the risk of lead violations. I cannot afford a 37% increase in employees nor can I force 40 employees to do the work of 64. Neither alternative can be achieved."[5]

Moreover, the paranoia is catching:

"One customer cancelled a $5,000 custom rock order after deciding that rocks were too 'dangerous' for a geology lesson because of the CPSIA lead rules and elected to use posters instead," said Warring. "What caliber of young scientists are we nurturing in our country when we won't let students touch and feel the textures, densities and hues of naturally-occurring rocks in a classroom? After all, kids pick up rocks outside the classroom every day. Our laws are scaring schools away from common sense choices about how our kids are educated."

Then there's Jolie Fay, of SkippingHippos.com, a one-woman operation that makes craft sewing kits. She ignored the warnings that CPSIA would affect her because, after all, why would it? Then she found out that she had to get her products tested, because some were sold to children. The truth dawned:

I called the lab, got the quote and did the math. CPSIA-mandated testing costs for my little product line was over $27,000 for just over $30,000 worth of product. I cannot express the horrible feeling I had when I realized that I had made a mistake that was going to cost my family all of our money. In the business world, companies recover. In my case, I WAS the company and what family can recover from a loss that huge? I was not only losing my investment, but I was also losing my source of income.[6]

What about the bureaucrats at CPSC, whose budget was almost doubled to administer this law? Could they help her? "The days passed, the fight went on. I would ask these aides and CPSC staffers 'what do I do? Should I just throw it all away?' and their response would be 'I cannot tell you what to do.' I was begging for help and they would only give me 'I cannot tell you what to do.'"

Eventually the CPSC issued some clarifications, exemptions and delays, but these were widely acknowledged as inadequate.

If you ever thought that progressives wanted to send history down the memory hole, you might be right, because another aspect of the law was it prohibited old books from being sold to or used by children. If the Nazis had their bonfires of forbidden books, so too does the modern bureaucrat—anything old is bad. As Elizabeth Mullaney Nicol wrote in *The New Atlantis*:

> The act defines its mission so broadly as to cover all "children's products," including children's books. The Consumer Product Safety Commission (CPSC), the agency charged with enforcement, issued guidelines days before CPSIA was to take effect in February 2009 specifying that all children's books published before 1985 would become illegal to sell unless they passed a lead-content test: less than 600 parts per million, dropping down to 300 ppm in August 2009 and 90 ppm in 2011. Prior to 1985, lead in miniscule amounts was a common ingredient in ink (useful for its plasticity and softness). But lead is hazardous only when ingested. As Jay Dempsey of the Centers for Disease Control and Prevention told the Associated Press, "on a scale of one to ten, this is like a 0.5 level of concern." Eight-year-olds do not eat their books, there is no evidence that any child has ever been harmed by spending vast amounts of time with nineteenth- and twentieth-century books (certainly not the diminished intelligence associated

with lead poisoning!), and the loss we'd suffer by following this directive would be enormous.

Booksellers face a $100,000 fine for passing on these books, even giving them away.

The only solution was to throw them away. One person Mullaney quotes saw this happening:

> I just came back from my local thrift store with tears in my eyes! I watched as boxes and boxes of children's books were thrown into the garbage! Today was the deadline and I just can't believe it! Every book they had on the shelves prior to 1985 was destroyed! I managed to grab a 1967 edition of *The Outsiders* from the top of the box, but so many!

The CPSC's current advice to booksellers is that selling children's books printed before 1985 is okay, as long as they aren't sold to or for children! I'm not kidding:

> Used vintage children's books and other children's products sold as collector's items would not be primarily intended for children. Because of their value and age, they would not be expected to be used by children. Therefore, they do not fall into the definition of children's product and do not need to comply with the lead limits.

The image arises of gangs of scholarly kids hanging around outside bookstores asking passing adults if they will go in and buy them a copy of Glanville Downey's *Stories from Herodotus*.

Just to make things worse, the CPSC has also determined that just because you lend a book rather than sell it doesn't exempt you from the CPSIA. This means that libraries don't know what to do with their pre-1985 volumes. Having to dispose of them would decimate their collections, but one CPSC Commissioner told libraries that they should indeed "sequester" those books. The CPSC still admits that it cannot "categorically exempt older children's books in libraries...from the CPSIA lead ban,"[7] and even told Henry Waxman that. At the moment, the status of these collections remains in question, but it is not impossible that the CPSC might require libraries to destroy books that it cannot sell to collectors. All this has been done to prevent a threat that apparently doesn't exist (though of course that's the point: regulations like this are always more about employing the regulators, with your tax dollars, than they are about anything else). If there is any documented case of a child suffering lead-related illness contracted via ink in a children's book, I have yet to find it.[8] The CPSC—however much its hands are tied by a badly written statute—is using your money to kill off harmless businesses and ban children's books.

The EPA Conquers America

It's bad enough that Congress keeps churning out oppressive, government-enriching regulation. But sometimes bureaucrats even "tailor" laws to give themselves powers that Congress didn't intend them to have. That's what's happening with the Environmental Protection Agency (EPA), which asserts it can alter the plain meaning of the Clean Air Act in order to regulate greenhouse gases.

The EPA announced in 2009 that greenhouse gases endanger human health and welfare. That finding paved the way for a huge power grab by EPA bureaucrats. It could lead to the EPA's complete regulatory control over the nation's energy supply and its use.

Large apartment buildings and hospitals will need EPA operating permits to continue running their furnaces. Everything from your lawnmower to the local TV station's traffic helicopter will be regulated for fuel economy. The EPA could close the nation's power plants, send electricity prices skyrocketing, and be responsible for rolling blackouts. All for our own good of course—and on our dime. If you wanted to design an anti-stimulus package, you'd be hard-pressed to top this.

The EPA already holds massive power to stop energy projects. It has used its regulatory powers to hold up the construction of new coal, gas, nuclear, and even renewable-energy power plants and electricity-transmission lines around the country. Literally hundreds of viable energy projects, and thousands of private sector jobs, are at this very moment held up by regulatory delay.

But that's just part of the problem. The EPA's claim that it is obliged to regulate carbon dioxide (CO_2) as a pollutant will oblige it to impose costly, time-consuming permitting requirements on tens of thousands of previously unregulated small businesses and millions of previously unregulated entities. Even the EPA recognizes this danger, warning that its permitting programs could crash under their own weight, halting construction projects and leaving millions of firms in legal limbo. So it is trying to rewrite the law it says it has to enforce—and all for its own convenience. Whether this legal trickery will survive legal challenge is doubtful, but the bad news is, if the law the EPA says it has to enforce isn't rewritten, the result will be a vastly expanded EPA budget and staff and the blocking of about every construction and energy project you can imagine. It's a win-win scenario for the EPA and a lose-lose scenario for the rest of us.

Who Watches the Watchmen?

All the while EPA tells us what a great job it is doing in protecting our—and our children's health—you might wonder how the Obama administration validates its claims. The answer is simple: it asks EPA! The agency doesn't just draft and enforce regulations, it measures its own performance. That's how it can get away with absurd assertions like the one that says enforcement of the Clean Air Act provides $30 in benefits for every $1 in costs. Indeed, EPA boss Lisa Jackson told Congress that EPA should be able to regulate greenhouse gases precisely because it has a forty-year history of delivering trillions of dollars of benefits to the nation.

Yet when independent scholars look at these claims, they find the numbers just don't add up. For instance, economist Garrett Vaughn found that the EPA's claim of massive benefits from the Clean Air Act derives from a bunch of accounting tricks.[9] They claim that manufacturers who are forced to put up their prices because of EPA rules simply pass on these costs to the customer, so they bear no cost themselves. It appears that the EPA economists have never heard of the Law of Demand: when price goes up, demand falls. Similarly, the EPA assumes compliance costs of $0.00 after a very short time, which allows for a literally infinite benefit to cost ratio.

Because the EPA generates its fantastical benefits numbers, it has ample justification for imposing yet more costly regulation on the American public. It follows that anyone who opposes these new rules obviously wants to poison the air.

No one in government questions these numbers, because that would stop the inexorable move towards more government. Yet, as economists Richard Belzer and Randall Lutter commented about EPA's year 2000 cost-benefit report:

> The same agencies that evaluate performance also design and administer the very regulatory programs they are evaluating. It is hard to understand why anyone should expect self-examinations to be objective and informative. Investors want businesses to be audited by analysts without financial conflicts of interest. Scientists reject research that cannot be replicated independently. Consumers flock to independent testing organizations rather than rely exclusively on sellers' claims. Only in the public sector, where bureaucrats are

protected from the discipline of market forces, do we rely on self-evaluations of performance.[10]

Until we do something to stop these outrageous, evidence-free claims of effectiveness by the EPA and other government agencies, government will keep on growing. At the moment, we are stuck somewhere between the Emperor with No Clothes and Orwell's *Animal Farm*. Only those are allegories, and this is real life.

PART THREE

ROBBER BARONS IN ACTION

CHAPTER SIX

PRIVATE SECTOR JARGON, PUBLIC SECTOR PERFORMANCE

The late Senator Daniel Patrick Moynihan once commented, "The single most exciting thing you encounter in government is competence, because it's so rare." Or as Sir Humphrey Appleby put it in *Yes Minister*, when confronted with a desire for greater public oversight to reduce waste, "The public doesn't know anything about wasting government money, we're the experts."

The big government we pay for might be called "the managerial state." It is a philosophy that government managers bring reason and order to an otherwise chaotic marketplace, and that the man in the bureaucrat's chair really does know better. But while the government managers put themselves above the private sector as its regulators, they like to appropriate and ape its claims for efficiency and production. But an important difference is that efficiency in the private sector lowers the costs of goods and services we want to buy. In government, the manager wants his "business," the bureaucracy, to grow as well. In his case, though, it's all on our dime doing things that stifle the private sector and increase the national debt.

The central question we should ask about bureaucracy is not how well the bureaucrats are performing, but why they are doing things at all. For instance, a bureaucrat at the Department of Health and Human Services might boast about expanding new sex education programs to elementary schools nationwide; but the key question is not how successful he was at doing that, but should the federal government really be doing that in the first place?

TSA:
Thousands Standing Around

The most famous—and failed—attempts at managerialism are in nationalized industries, where bureaucratic managers act as if they can make better, more rational decisions than businessmen can. A spectacular recent example of the government taking over a private sector function and making it worse is airport security. After the disaster of 9/11, everyone in politics agreed we needed a change from the previously privately operated airport security system, and so the Transportation Security Administration was born.

The result was a massive increase in visible airline security. Every domestic passenger had to go through personal security screening, with particular attention being paid to potential instruments of terror. Initially, this concentrated on sharp objects, because the hijackers of 9/11 had used boxcutters. So nail clippers and small scissors were routinely removed from traveling grandmothers.

Then in December 2001 came Richard Reid, who attempted to blow up an airliner on the Paris to Miami route with a makeshift bomb (that he attempted to light with a match) hidden in his hollowed-out shoes. The private French security service at Charles de Gaulle airport had in fact stopped Reid from boarding the flight the day before owing to his disheveled appearance and suspicious behavior. It was the French police force that issued a boarding pass for the flight he eventually took. Owing to the day's delay, he was unable to get his bomb to work, and he was tackled by other passengers and then sedated by a traveling doctor. As a result of the "shoe bomber" case, the TSA decided, unlike other security authorities around the world, that all passengers would henceforth be required to remove their shoes. Ironically, the particular explosive Reid used, PETN, cannot be detected by scanners, but only by a chemical test.[1]

Within a few years, security analysts were aware that potential terrorists were considering less direct means to attack airliners. Yet the TSA dismissed the idea. Freelance writer Becky Akers takes up the story:

> The TSA had gone from bad to worse [by 2004] when undercover investigators packed their bags with common household items that explode when combined. They tried to smuggle these ingredients past the checkpoints at 21 airports—and they succeeded every time.
>
> Barraged by criticism, DHS pooh-poohed the test's premises: "While random items commonly found under a kitchen sink could conceivably be concocted into an IED [improvised explosive device], we find it highly implausible."
>
> Months later, British police announced that they had foiled a plot to smuggle explosive components aboard planes, combine them en route, and blow up 10 transatlantic flights. That "highly implausible" scenario now has American passengers bagging their gels and liquids like tuna sandwiches.[2]

Then, on Christmas Day 2009, the "underwear bomber" made his attempt. Concealing some PETN in his underwear, Umar Farouk Abdulmutallab attempted to ignite the explosive on a flight from Amsterdam to Detroit. Once again, he was foiled by passengers (not before suffering burns to his leg and genitalia). Thankfully, the TSA did not start demanding that passengers remove their underwear.

They did the next best thing, though, and speeded up the introduction of "backscatter" X-ray machines designed to look through passengers' clothing. These "nudie scanners" unsurprisingly led to a hail of protest, and the TSA allowed an "opt-out" that consisted of an intrusive "enhanced pat-down," which involves TSA agents feeling your underwear region and other areas quite intimately.

As former FAA security agent Steve Elson says in the devastating 2010 documentary about the TSA, *Please Remove Your Shoes*, "They focus on all kinds of minutiae and crap, rather than the items they need to." Elson relates one particularly revealing story about the time a fake explosive device was sent into a scanner with an ordinary bottle of water placed right next to it. The security agents detected the water and removed it. They ignored the bomb entirely.

It should now be quite clear that the TSA is a reactive security operation, always fighting the last battle. Yet it doesn't even fight those battles particularly well. Whenever the TSA's performance has been measured, it has been found woefully inadequate. In fact, TSA checks regularly miss dummy explosives used by testers to discover inadequacies in the system. As *USA Today* reported in 2007, a suppressed government report shows that TSA airports are much more likely to fail to detect a bomb than the one major airport in the United States that still uses private screeners:

> Screeners at Los Angeles International Airport missed about 75% of simulated explosives and bomb parts that Transportation Security Administration testers hid under their clothes or in carry-on bags at checkpoints, the TSA report shows.
>
> At Chicago O'Hare International Airport, screeners missed about 60% of hidden bomb materials that were packed in everyday carry-ons including toiletry kits, briefcases and CD players. San Francisco International Airport screeners, who work for a private company instead of the TSA, missed about

20% of the bombs, the report shows. The TSA ran about 70 tests at Los Angeles, 75 at Chicago and 145 at San Francisco.[3]

The leaks to *USA Today* also suggest that TSA screeners are less efficient than the pre-9/11 arrangements:

> Tests earlier in 2002 showed screeners missing 60% of fake bombs. In the late 1990s, tests showed that screeners missed about 40% of fake bombs, according to a separate report by the Government Accountability Office, the investigative arm of Congress.

As for why the private San Francisco screeners should be more vigilant than their TSA-employed counterparts, the TSA report acknowledged that San Francisco screeners know they will be picked on with constant covert tests and are therefore "more suspicious."

All of which suggests that, as the producers of *Please Remove Your Shoes* assert, we are worse off today in security terms than we were prior to 9/11 (and we weren't in particularly good shape then, to put it mildly). Ever since Libyan state-sponsored terrorists blew up Pan Am Flight 103 over Lockerbie, Scotland, killing 270 people, the FAA and then the TSA have sponsored a "Red Team," which attempts to think like terrorists to probe airports' security operations. Since 2003, it has tested 735 airports, using proxies that should detect as if they were actual explosives.

One of the film's principals, Bogdan Dzakovic, told the Denver CBS affiliate what the Red Team's findings at Denver International Airport meant:

> Sources told 9NEWS the Red Team was able to sneak about 90 percent of simulated weapons past checkpoint screeners in Denver. In the baggage area, screeners caught one explosive device that was packed in a suitcase. However later, screeners in the baggage area missed a book bomb, according to sources.

"There's very little substance to security," said former Red Team leader Bogdan Dzakovic. "It literally is all window dressing that we're doing. It's big theater on TV and when you go to the airport. It's just security theater."[4]

How was Dzakovic in a position to know this?

Dzakovic was a Red Team leader from 1995 until September 11, 2001. After the terrorist attacks, Dzakovic became a federally protected whistleblower and alleged that thousands of people died needlessly. He testified before the 9/11 Commission and the National Commission on Terrorist Attacks Upon the US that the Red Team "breached security with ridiculous ease up to 90 percent of the time," and said the FAA "knew how vulnerable aviation security was."

Dzakovic, who is currently a TSA inspector, said security is no better today.

"It's worse now. The terrorists can pretty much do what they want when they want to do it," he said.

When CBS said Dzakovic was "currently a TSA inspector," it was slightly overstating the case. After complaining that the Red Team's findings prior to 9/11 had been covered up, he was transferred to a desk job at the TSA:

After filing his complaint, Dzakovic was removed from his Red Team leadership position. He now works for the Transportation Security Administration, which has responsibility for airport security. His primary assignments include tasks such as hole-punching, updating agency phonebooks and "thumb-twiddling," he says. At least he hasn't received a pay cut, he says. He makes about $110,000 a year for what he describes as "entry-level idiot work."[5]

All of which raises the question as to why the creation of the TSA led to worse performance. The answer comes down to managerialism. The TSA was initially composed lock, stock, and barrel of employees who had previously worked for the Federal Aviation Administration, which had overseen the previous, obviously faulty, pre-9/11 regime. Their reward was actually a vast increase in power and budget. They elbowed aside their former contractors to manage security directly, and thereby worsened performance, by taking a failed model, building on it, and turning it into a mature bureaucracy dedicated to its own continuance. Moreover, it is the very nature of politics and political bureaucracy to operate not by a model of efficiency but by a model of CYA (cover your you-know-what). That is why airport security is all about going through an elaborate routine, regardless of its lack of effectiveness, just so if something goes wrong the bureaucrats can claim to have done everything possible, from making us take off our shoes to going through nude body scanners. Of course, given more funding and a larger staff, they could do even better!

Or actually, they wouldn't. As my colleague Hans Bader points out, even in European countries run by Socialist parties, airline security and screening is generally in the hands of private companies, which means it is usually more diligent, innovative, and efficient, less bureaucratic, and a lot less burdensome on the average traveler.

But alas, here in freedom-loving America, the TSA bureaucracy is now entrenched and expanding its powers. John Pistole, the current head of the Transportation Security Administration, told *The Atlantic* in a 2010 interview that "we'll never eliminate risk" of terrorist attacks on aviation. He's right on that, but it's exactly why the TSA's policy of treating every passenger as a potential terrorist is so misguided. It is the most inefficient way imaginable to meet a terrorist threat.

It has also given TSA officers power without responsibility, which became apparent during the litany of horror stories that spawned a backlash against the X-ray screenings and pat-downs. Some of these stories win more ink than others because they sound like *Saturday Night Live* sketches, as in the case of the former Baywatch actress who was singled out for additional screening. The case of the Baywatch actress is particularly interesting because of the TSA's response to the controversy. An agency spokesman said that "people who are celebrities shouldn't be surprised if and when they're recognized." This makes no sense. If they're recognized as not terrorists, then why should they have to go through enhanced security without additional information that they may be a threat? Perhaps terrorist "chatter" that day suggested that a former Baywatch star might be planning a midair atrocity, but I seriously doubt it. Actually, I have no doubt that she was singled out for screening precisely because she was attractive and the officers had the power to do it. Because we, the traveling public—even celebrities—have so little recourse, TSA officers get away with stuff that would be firing offenses in many jobs.[6]

More airports should be allowed to hire their own private security personnel, not only because they appear to do a better job, but to give the TSA a little competition. But that's not the way big government operates. Instead, the opposite is going to happen—and worse is to follow.

On February 4, 2011, the Obama administration gave TSA officials the right to unionize the agency's workforce. This means that, if TSA officers vote for it, up to 50,000 new union members will be paying hefty union dues—possibly $30 million annually, with the bill paid for by the taxpayers who fund their salaries. For travelers, this will likely mean longer lines and even less responsive officials, because it is ridiculously difficult to fire a unionized government employee (as we'll see in the next chapter). And the taxes we pay for being harassed by TSA staff will escalate in line with escalating union pay scales that rely more on seniority and bureaucratic job title classifications than on performance.

Safety could also be compromised. As Republican Senator Roger Wicker of Mississippi, who is attempting to ban collective bargaining rights with a legislative amendment, says, "It's no different from FBI agents or Secret Service agents. [TSA agents are] protected in other ways, but the union contracts and the demands of collective bargaining are cumbersome and less flexible than what we need in national security situations."

TSA Administrator John Pistole asserts that there will be no collective bargaining on security-related issues—for an agency whose middle name is "Security." In fact, airline security is the TSA's *entire* mission, not acting as a conduit for channeling taxpayer money to unions.

Republican Congressman John L. Mica of Florida, one of the authors of the legislation that created the TSA and now Chairman of the House Transportation and Infrastructure Committee, has proposed ending the agency's near monopoly on airport screening.

"When the TSA was established, it was never envisioned that it would become a huge, unwieldy bureaucracy which was soon to grow to 67,000 employees," wrote Congressman Mica in a 2010 letter to the heads of more than 150 airports. "As TSA has grown larger, more impersonal, and administratively top-heavy, I believe it is important that airports across the country consider utilizing the opt-out provision provided by law."

This makes it especially unfortunate that the TSA is trying its hardest to render the opt-out provision moot—even as it remains on the books. On January 24, the agency announced that it "is still accepting applications [for opt-outs], but unless a clear and substantial advantage to do so emerges in the future, the requests will not be approved."

Pistole said publicly that he doesn't believe such an advantage exists, a belief that conflicts with the findings of official studies—which the TSA tried to suppress—that compared TSA operations unfavorably with those of private operators.

Congressman Mica disagrees with Pistole's assessment. "Past studies have indicated that private screening operations' performance is equal to, or 'statistically significantly better than' the all-federal operations," he says. "Furthermore, almost all of the positive innovations that have been adopted by the TSA in the screening process have emanated from private screening operations."

The TSA denied Springfield-Branson National Airport in Missouri the option to use private contractors. Airport spokesman Kent Boyd is confident, however, that a private company would be able to improve the customer service offered at the airport. "While a private company is still under the supervision of TSA, the screeners are employees of a private company," Boyd said. "If there's a problem, the airport can go directly to the company to seek a resolution," a process that "tends not to happen with the TSA."

Private screeners, however, are harder to unionize than government employees—and government employees make up a majority of all union members, a key Obama constituency. As government employees become a more and more lopsided majority of union members, their pressure to increase the size of the bureaucracy will grow. That is bad news for taxpayers.

Airports like Springfield have no recourse—and the same is, unfortunately, true for travelers. When it comes to the TSA, it's the union way or the highway.

Only the Government Can Do It!

The thing to remember is that the government takes your money on the pretext that it is competent enough to do things you care about and that it can do them better than the private sector. For the most part, it isn't, it can't, and you are being swindled.

Yet the idea that government funding somehow improves our economy remains commonplace. For example, it is commonly argued and accepted that government has to take some of our money and invest it for us in scientific research, because without the government doing it, no one will. This argument is usually followed up with the supposed knock-down argument that the United States government created the Internet, possibly with an approving reference to Al Gore.

This argument is the main reason government spends so much on grants and research contracts. Many thousands of people are employed indirectly by government at research institutions on large salaries (as we'll see in the education chapter) at public expense. In turn, they demand more grants, increased funding, and more researchers.

The idea that government had to be involved in scientific research really got started with Vannevar Bush, President Franklin D. Roosevelt's top science adviser, and gained credence because of the need for military-driven research in World War II and, later, the Cold War. Bush believed that government investment in science led directly to results that led to commercial applications that led to an improved economy, and that one couldn't rely on private industry to fund "basic research." This was Vannevar's theory, but in fact, as Adam Smith had long before demonstrated, most technological advances actually arise within industry; Smith noted that flying shuttle, the spinning jenny, the spinning frame, Arkwright's water frame, and Crompton's mule— all of the major inventions that were prompting industrial growth in the eighteenth century—were developed within industry by skilled industrial craftsmen. Smith rejected the idea that applied sciences should be supported by the state, because market forces did a much more efficient job.[7]

Yes, you say, but that was the eighteenth century; Vannevar Bush was dealing with the challenges of the atomic age (which he helped usher in). But Smith's faith in the market, rather than government, as the driver of most technological advances has been vindicated by empirical studies covering the 1960s, 1970s, and the mid-1980s, which showed that only about 10 percent of industrial advances required academic research. Moreover, it turned out that American companies routinely invested in pure science and that those that invested the most made the greatest gains in productivity and profits.[8] So even after government became a major investor in science, it was industry that was driving technological innovation and progress. More than that, industrial innovations have propelled the pure sciences. Terence Kealey, vice chancellor of the University of Buckingham, points out that entire fields such as radio-astronomy, ceramic superconductivity, and molecular biology arose—at least in part—out of developments which were made in industrial labs (such as Bell Labs) as well as privately-funded research institutes (such as the Rockefeller Institute).

Government support of science is simply not necessary. Research would not suddenly cease if its government subsidies were cut. In fact, if commensurate cuts were made in corporate and capital gains taxes, it is likely that businesses would invest *more* in research. Government is singularly ill-suited for promoting scientific research, because it is driven by political rather than practical considerations—and politicians, as a rule, are both bad judges of commercial opportunity and ignorant in science. The trouble with the argument that only government can adequately support ambitious, long-term scientific projects like the Internet or CERN (the European Organization for Nuclear Research) is that it rests on the risible assumption that politicians are somehow best placed to make balanced, disinterested judgments about what scientific research should be funded. Politicians might claim and sincerely believe they are working to serve the "public interest," but experience teaches us that what really drive political decisions are special interest groups and electoral constituencies. The goal in politics is to get reelected, and large projects are almost inevitably awarded as pork barrel grants (regardless of actual need), or out of a nationalistic fear of "falling behind" other governments in funding science. The bureaucrats who control the funding pipelines have their own corporate interests: namely seeking larger budgets, hiring more employees, and forging ties between themselves and the special interests. Bureaucrats who take unpopular stands may later find it difficult to secure lucrative positions in the private sector.

Not only are their motives not as pure as advertised, government officials have historically been inept at judging commercial opportunity, as the heady pace of technological development frequently renders grandiose projects redundant before they are even completed. European governments wasted huge sums of money in the early 1990s to improve domestic electronic manufacturing among a host of firms you've never heard of, while IBM, Intel, Texas Instruments, and Apple all flourished without equivalent government assistance.

Not only is government ineffective at managing scientific investment, its attempts to do so harm the very industries it claims to promote. Government assists industry when it creates an environment conducive to business (by providing stable political conditions, the rule of law, low tax rates, and so on). But we should remember that actual wealth is *always* generated by the private sector, not government. As Henry Hazlitt points out, it is foolish to think that government can create "wealth" by borrowing money and "investing" it into the economy, since the debt will eventually have to be repaid. Printing additional money creates inflation, which harms businesses and individuals, depreciating the value of their savings, and creating an uncertain economic environment. Because government is ill-suited to make the best economic investments, it is unlikely that it will ever rake back enough in taxes (from an economy supposedly stimulated by government investment) to pay back the debt.

Subsidies must be paid for, and government can only raise money through taxation. Regardless of whether they hit businesses directly, hit consumers first (reducing their purchasing power), or are postponed (by governments taking on debt), taxes increase the costs of doing business while reducing profits and capital (which would otherwise fund more jobs and more research). It is simply incoherent to argue that science must be publicly funded in order to help industry. As Terence Kealey puts it, "To tax industry to enable government to subsidize it must, in general terms, be absurd." We'd all be better off if government conceded it had no role in subsidizing scientific research—and the very fact that it is virtually impossible for us to imagine such a concession only underlines the point about what government-funded research is all about: increasing the size and scope, wealth and power of the political class.

Incompetence and Fraud

In the private sector, incompetence is generally punished and fraud is generally prosecuted. Not so in government. The U.S. Department of Agriculture (USDA) is one of the oldest redoubts of big government we have. Aside from the inherent wastefulness of the department—famously paying farmers not to grow crops—the USDA has become a funnel for money to what we might call "farm fraud."

In 1997, a black farmer named Timothy Pigford and 400 other black farmers sued the USDA, alleging discrimination in the USDA's processing of loan applications.[9] Pigford asked that an estimated 2,000 African American victims who "farmed or attempted to farm" be included in the lawsuit,[10] and a judge certified the suit as a class action encompassing all black farmers who had filed an antidiscrimination complaint against the USDA between the years 1983 and 1997.

In 1999, the parties settled. Under the terms of the settlement, all African American claimants would be awarded $50,000 on the production of minimal evidence, together with tax offsets and loan forgiveness. This avenue for reparation was known as "Track A," while there was also a "Track B" with the promise of potentially higher reparations for being able to present a preponderance of evidence of discrimination. Claimants were to file within 180 days, although claims were accepted up to a year later in the event of extraordinary circumstances delaying the filing.

Far from the original expectation of 2,000 claims, the figure exploded to 22,721 claimants, nearly 16,000 of whom received considerable financial rewards (almost all received the $50,000 plus non-credit awards and debt relief, with only 200 opting for the Track B procedure), leading to a cost to the USDA of *more than $1 billion*.

There were a further 70,000 claims filed too late. These claimants argued that they did not have enough notice of the settlement. A provision in the 2008 Farm Bill allowed what amounted to a rehearing of their claims in civil court. This was backed by an additional $1.15 billion for settling what came to be called *Pigford II*. This might sound like a typical case of a bureaucracy messing up and having to pay out taxpayers' money as a result. But the extraordinary number of claims suggests that something far worse is afoot.

Republican Congressman Steve King of Iowa, a member of both the House Agriculture and the House Judiciary Committees, sent a letter on September 24, 2010, to Agriculture Secretary Tom Vilsack requesting a meeting to discuss allegations of major fraud in the disbursement of Pigford settlement money. He wrote:

> There is a growing firestorm over the allegations of massive fraud in the Pigford settlement....According to sworn testimony by John Boyd, President of the National Black Farmers Association, there are 18,000 black farmers. They could not all have been victims of discrimination. To date, there have been over 94,000 claims made. These numbers speak to massive fraud, meaning that American taxpayers are on the hook for what Pigford judge Paul Friedman called "forty acres and a mule."[11]

Journalist Andrew Breitbart of BigGovernment.com estimates that the settlement involves "anywhere between 75- and 95-percent fraud":

> There were 18,000 black farmers in the country in the '90s. Now there are 94,000 people getting claims. There's more people getting claims upwards of $87,000 per person—

getting money from the government—allegedly for having
been discriminated against as a black farmer. But these people
had never seen a piece of farmland in their entire lives, they
were just given money for claiming that they were farmers.[12]

Even under the most generous estimates of the number of black farmers
who could be eligible for a Pigford settlement, "the numbers," as Andrew
Breitbart says, "don't add up."[13]

The anecdotal evidence seems to support this conclusion as well.
Writes Breitbart,

> One of the key Pigford class action attorneys based out of
> Pine Bluff, Arkansas admits that many of his own clients
> "got away with murder." Othello Cross, who is the key
> Pigford attorney in Arkansas, the state with the third most
> claimants, and who represents hundreds of [individuals] who
> received at least $50,000 from the U.S. taxpayer, admits on
> video that at least 10% of his clients—that he knows of—
> defrauded the government.[14]

In Cross's experience, it wasn't at all difficult for individuals to fraudu-
lently fill out the paperwork, especially if they had any awareness of the
terminology used by farmers. "If they had been sharecropping—
if they had been working on a person's farm—they knew all the language
that you need to know to file a valid claim. So most of them would be
the children of farmers, of sharecroppers—or they had sharecropped
themselves."[15]

It seems that "sounding good" was all you needed to get money from
the government. Othello Cross confirmed this, claiming that there
"wasn't anything you could do about it. How are you gonna check them?
All that they have to say is 'I attempted to farm…I went out, and the
man told me there was no more money, all the money had run out,' or

'the man just told me to get out.'"[16] The potential for fraud is especially prevalent because, according to Cross, *USDA agents didn't even keep records of loan applications.*

There's little doubt the USDA messed up badly and some black farmers were caused financial difficulty. But how many were truly discriminated against? Former Agriculture Secretary Ed Schafer is extremely worried: "I am concerned that the legislated validation process has now been overlooked and our Government has agreed to settle all claims without proper investigation of the potential fraud and abuse.... The allegations of fraud and abuse must be addressed if we are going to assure our citizens that their government is pursuing equal justice for all."[17]

The *Washington Times* reports that some black farmers have complained about the process to their Congressional representative, only to be given the bum's rush:

> Numerous black farmers have complained they get short shrift while grifters and lawyers get the loot. In January [2011], these websites posted videos of black farmers saying they brought fraud concerns to Rep. Sanford Bishop, Georgia Democrat, but he advised them to stay quiet "as long as the money was flowing" because otherwise "they'll shut this thing down." Three men—including Eddie Slaughter, vice president of the Black Farmers and Agriculturalists Association—agree Mr. Bishop said this in his Columbus, Ga., office.
>
> "Yes, I am aware that there is fraud in the program, that's why anti-fraud provisions were written into the settlement," Mr. Bishop stated, according to the Jan. 20 Albany (Ga.) Herald. "It's not my job to monitor fraud in the program."[18]

The USDA first hurt black farmers, and now it is hurting the taxpayers. And what is the reward for the USDA's incompetence? In 1980, the federal government spent about $9 billion on agriculture.[19]

In February 2011, the president requested a budget of $145 billion for the USDA.[20]

The Reverend Moon
Would Be Proud

If government behaves this badly, why do we put up with it? It's because government counts on our apathy, successfully plays interest groups against each other, and has rebranded itself as a disinterested agent of good (while it is anything but). But if the government is made up of angels who look after the public, it follows that there have to be demons they protect us from—and according to the self-justifying government myth, those demons reside in the private sector. They include tobacco companies, oil and coal companies, and auto makers; soon, perhaps, they'll be joined by fast food franchises and soda companies. What usually happens is that the bureaucracy targets an industry and threatens to regulate it. To stave off Draconian government punishments, the industry cooperates with the bureaucracy—to the taxpayers' detriment. The industry gets to help the regulator write the new regulations, and the regulator gets to oversee the industry. A revolving door opens and the industry and the bureaucratic agency regularly swap personnel. Among economists this is known as "regulatory capture."

At the basest level, individual bureaucrats can get the benefits of petty corruption—favors, junkets, perhaps even the odd bribe, and the prospect of a high-paying industry job with the industry when they leave government. At the middling level, this is one of the processes by which the bureaucracy grows—expanding the scope of its regulations means more power, higher budgets, and more bureaucrats. At the highest level, administrators of the agencies, who often are politicians or have political ambitions, are able to extract campaign contributions or donations from the industry to favored groups.

Of course, this cozy relationship means bureaucrats often fail to do their purported jobs. A pointed example came in the Deepwater Horizon oil spill, which revealed that BP and the Minerals Management Service (MMS) worked hand in glove. As Gerry O'Driscoll of the Cato Institute wrote in the *Wall Street Journal*:

> By all accounts, MMS operated as a rubber stamp for BP. It is a striking example of regulatory capture: Agencies tasked with protecting the public interest come to identify with the regulated industry and protect its interests against that of the public. The result: Government fails to protect the public. That conclusion is precisely the same for the financial services industry.
>
> Financial services have long been subject to detailed regulation by multiple agencies. In his book on the financial crisis, *Jimmy Stewart Is Dead*, Boston University Professor Laurence Kotlikoff counts over 115 regulatory agencies for financial services. If more hands in the pot helped, financial services would be in fine shape. Few believe such is the case.[21]

Regulatory capture is great for the industry, which gains a privileged position against its competitors, great for the bureaucrats, who can feather their nests, and great for politicians, who tell the public they're protecting them while also getting the benefits of industry money. But of course it's taxpayers that get stuck with the bill, and smaller businesses that get regulated out of the market.

What about industries that fight the regulators' power grab? That's where the demonization comes in. Because regulators are allegedly on the side of the public, the industry is immediately cast as an enemy, more interested in greedy profits than the public interest. That's a pr battle most industries can't win, even if it's not really business that lives by that motto "greed is good"—businesses have to produce a wanted product to earn money. It's the government bureaucracy, which has no limit on its ravenous appetite to feast on our tax dollars, producing no product that we asked for and taking over more and more control of our economy and our lives.

CHAPTER SEVEN

UNION MEN

Even Samuel Gompers, the founding president of the American Federation of Labor (AFL), knew that unions weren't for everyone. He once said, "There may be here and there a worker who for certain reasons unexplainable to us does not join a union of labor. This is his right, no matter how morally wrong he may be. It is his legal right and no one can or dare question his exercise of that legal right."[1]

Today only 7 percent of private sector workers are union members. But government workers are a different story.

According to the Bureau of Labor Statistics, there are 22.2 million government workers in the United States. Almost 7.6 million of them are unionized, compared with only 7.1 million in the private sector. The largest member union of the AFL-CIO is the American Federation of State, Council and Municipal Employees (AFSCME), with 1.5 million members. Other large government sector unions include the federal-level American Federation of Government Employees (AFGE) with 600,000 members and the Service Employees International Union (SEIU) with 1.9 million members (not all of them government employees). The National Education Association, which represents public school teachers, university faculty, and others involved in education (including retirees), has 3.2 million members.

What makes union involvement in government so pernicious is that public sector unions dictate salary levels (which are much higher than they are in the private sector), platinum-plated benefits packages (ditto), and working standards and conditions that, famously, make it almost impossible to fire a government employee no matter how bad his performance. If the political class is stealing you blind, labor unions are the Thieves' Guild.

Snow Job

In December 2010, New York City was pounded by a massive blizzard. But the city's sanitation employees allegedly decided to clear the streets on a slow-motion schedule as a demonstration of union strength. The consequence was that these "public servants" left people to die, as ambulances couldn't navigate the snowed-in streets.

Luis Reynoso, whose three-month-old son died en route to the hospital, had no doubt about why his son was not saved. He told the *New York Post*, "Clean the streets, because that's why the ambulance came too late."[2]

New York City Councilman Dan Halloran revealed shortly after the storm that he had been told by two separate sources that disgruntled union supervisors, annoyed at their likely demotion for budgetary reasons, had ordered their crews not to clean up the snow as quickly as they might.

"They sent a message to the rest of the city that these particular labor issues are more important," Halloran told FOX News. "[Sanitation workers] were told to take off routes [and] not do the plowing of some of the major arteries in a timely manner. They were told to make the mayor pay for the layoffs, the reductions in rank for the supervisors, [and] shrinking the rolls of the rank-and-file."

Further allegations surfaced. According to the *New York Post*:

> The selfish Sanitation bosses who sabotaged the blizzard cleanup to fire a salvo at City Hall targeted politically connected and well-heeled neighborhoods in Queens and Brooklyn to get their twisted message across loud and clear, *The Post* has learned....
>
> Sources told *The Post* several neighborhoods were on the workers' hit list—including Borough Park and Dyker Heights in Brooklyn and Middle Village in Queens—because residents there have more money and their politicians carry big sticks.
>
> "It was more targeted than people actually think," said a labor source. "Borough Park was specifically targeted [because of]...its ability to sort of gin up the p.r. machine."[3]

But even as some suffered, others were let off easy:

> Sources said Sanitation bosses issued verbal directives during the clean-up to give priority to streets near the homes of agency heads and other city bigwigs. "This happens all the time," one Sanit (*sic*) worker said. "They make sure the bosses and politicians get taken care of."[4]

The public was enraged:

> Moshe Pollack, 55, of Borough Park, said, "It's disgusting. And we pay them overtime for this? People could have died."
>
> John Delliliune, 42, of Penelope Avenue in Middle Village said he was "very disappointed" but "not surprised."

"I saw plows driving around with their shovels up," he fumed, adding, "I would like to see some disciplinary action to whoever made the call."

…Chaya Schron, who lives in Midwood, Brooklyn, said she didn't hear any plows passing by her bedroom window Sunday night or Monday morning.

"I suspected a slowdown from the very beginning. It didn't make sense," she said.

On Monday, she saw a plow drive down her street with its blade up.

"When we asked why his plow was up, he said he had instructions not to plow side streets because it wastes gas," she said. "I was in disbelief."[5]

And that wasn't the end of it. When the snow was finally cleared, the accumulated garbage bags were left uncollected, perhaps as another public-spirited act of thumbing one's nose at the taxpaying public.

The Coddled Public Sector

Overall, American government-union members today get paid more than the workers in the private sector, enjoy better benefits, and are increasingly exempt from laws that govern everyone else. Indeed, unions are actually bankrupting states with their lavish pay and benefit costs.

Public-sector unionism is a relatively recent phenomenon in the United States. In 1959, Wisconsin became the first state to allow its public employees to unionize. In 1962, President John F. Kennedy issued an executive order allowing federal employees to join unions. Since then, public sector unions have helped drive the movement for more expansive and expensive government. They use forced dues, garnished from wages paid by taxpayer money, to lobby for greater pay and better benefits.

The Center for Responsive Politics lists the American Federation of State, Council and Municipal Employees (AFSCME) as second on its list of all-time political donors. In the 2010 election, the 1.6-million-member organization spent almost $90 million—a stunning amount given that the union had only $97.4 million in assets in 2009. AFSCME was forced to use a $16 million emergency account and take out a $2 million loan to pay for its political activities. Before the election, Larry Scanlon, head of AFSCME's political operations, reinforced the weight of the union's political giving, saying: "We're the big dog." AFSCME president Gerald McEntee also commented on the size of the contributions: "We're spending big. And we're damn happy it's big. And our members are damn happy it's big—it's their money."

The National Education Association (NEA) is eighth on the all-time political donors list, the Service Employees International Union (SEIU) is eleventh, and the American Federation of Teachers (AFT) comes in at thirteenth. The NEA and AFT spent more than $75 million on politics and lobbying in the 2009 fiscal year alone. In short, public-sector unions constitute a permanent, well-funded, self-supporting lobby for bigger government. The teachers' unions' investment paid off in August 2010, when the House of Representatives reconvened to pass the Education Jobs Fund (in the Bill with No Name)—which added $10 billion to the $53.5 billion Congress had already approved to bail out unionized teachers.

The unions were gambling big on the Democrats' staying in control in Washington, because they had a lot at stake: the 2009 stimulus bill and other legislation passed by the Democrat-controlled Congress sent $160 billion in federal tax money to the states, much of it spent on shielding government-sector workers from layoffs.

According to OpenSecrets.org, the politician who received the largest donations from public sector unions in the 2010 congressional election cycle was an undistinguished lawmaker called Gerry Connolley. Mr. Connolley just happens to represent the Eleventh District of Virginia, which you may remember as America's Wealthiest District, just outside Washington, D.C. Interestingly, Mr. Connolley's largest individual donor was not a union, but a firm called SAIC, Inc., which relies almost exclusively, as far as I can make out, on government contracts for its income.[6]

Unions, both government and private, demand—and often get—exemptions from the laws and regulations government imposes on the rest of us. For instance, the UFT, the New York City chapter of the AFT, was the first of many unions to receive an exemption from the mandatory minimum of coverage imposed by Obamacare—a bill that, incidentally, the AFT supported.

The health-care law orders that companies that provide insurance must offer a minimum of $750,000 in coverage to each employee in 2011, $1.25 million in 2012, $2 million in 2013, and an unlimited amount by 2014. The law hurts businesses that offer small health-insurance plans known as mini-meds, mostly to hourly wage temporary workers. In some cases, premiums for these businesses could double. McDonald's, which employs thousands of hourly workers, has already announced that it will have to cut health-care benefits to workers because of the law. Other employers could well follow suit.

In response—and probably because, for political reasons, it did not want a million minimum-wage workers kicked off their health-care plans weeks before an election—the Obama administration granted 30 waivers in the beginning of October 2010; by mid-November that number grew to over 111. There are now thousands. The waivers are good for one year and cover about 1 million people. The largest initial waiver went not to a corporate giant like McDonald's, but to the UFT. It requested a waiver for the 351,000 members in its "welfare fund," which covers up to $100,000 for a member's prescriptions, while New York City covers hospital and primary-care-physician treatments for them and their families. Without the waiver, though, the union would need either to pay drastically increased premiums or cut the prescription-drug benefit.

The UFT lobbied heavily for the very health-care bill from which its president, Michael Mulgrew, then demanded an exemption. During the health-care debate, the New York State UFT website even featured a "myth vs. fact" advocacy piece promoting the health-care bill. Here's a sample:

> **Myth:** Health care reform will force you out of your current insurance plan or force you to change doctors.
>
> **Fact:** You can keep your existing insurance; reform will expand your medical options, not eliminate them.

It seems Mulgrew's staff got the myth and fact mixed up; without the waiver, the teachers could not have kept their existing insurance.

And this isn't the first time unions have received special treatment under Obamacare. The president's "compromise" with Big Labor exempted union health plans from the excise tax on high-end "Cadillac" plans until 2018.

Labor Day Is Pay Day

The real myth is that public sector labor unions represent low-paid employees who trade poor salaries for the security of good benefits. In fact, the public sector unions are fat cats, their union leaders claim huge salaries, and they operate on budgets that, if they were in the private sector, would qualify them as very large businesses. Let's start with the AFL-CIO's largest member, AFSCME. Its headquarters is at 1625 L Street NW, Washington, D.C., conveniently sited about half a mile from the White House. In 2009, it garnered about $202 million in income (about the same as YouTube's projected revenue for 2008, according to *Forbes* magazine) and spent just over that—$206 million. About a quarter of its spending—$48 million—was on politics. Its building is valued at about $18 million.

The AFSCME has 229 employees who get paid more than $100,000 a year. Of those, forty make over $150,000, ten make over $200,000, and four get over $250,000. The union's highest paid employees are William Lucy, the Secretary-Treasurer, who takes home $387,272, and the president, Gerald McEntee, who earns a whopping $479,328. That's almost a fifth as much again as the president of the United States. So the guy who represents public sector workers (with minimum dues of $16.20 a month) gets paid more than the most important public sector worker there is.

A few blocks away from where Mr. McEntee sits on top of his huge pile of cash is the headquarters of the National Education Association. Its building at 1201 16th Street NW (again about half a mile from the White House) is worth more than $110 million. The NEA spent $338 million in 2009, $50 million of it on politics.

The NEA has 214 employees making over $100,000 annually, 175 of them making over $150,000. No fewer than forty-two employees make $200,000 or more, with four making over $250,000. On top of the heap is John Wilson, Executive Director, who takes home $393,960. At least that's not as much as the president of the United States ($400,000).

How about the SEIU—the union that grew so big and powerful it withdrew from the AFL-CIO? It is headquartered in trendy Dupont Circle, but still less than a mile from the White House, in a building that cost just under $95 million. It raked in $316 million in 2009, and spent almost $60 million on politics (remember, all these figures are for 2009, a non-election year).

More than 200 SEIU employees take home in excess of $100,000 a year; thirty-six make more than $150,000; nine get paid more than $200,000; and four are recompensed more than $250,000. Andy Stern, the SEIU's influential and grandly styled "International President" cashed in to the tune of $306,388 in 2009. In 2010, Stern surprisingly took early retirement from the SEIU, presumably on generous terms, and joined private equity and biowarfare firms as an advisor.

Given the recent nationalization of Detroit's auto industry, we shouldn't forget the mighty Union of Automobile Workers, the UAW, headquartered in Detroit. The UAW has more retirees (600,000) than employed workers (390,000), on its membership rolls, making it essentially a highly specialized version of AARP. Despite having far fewer members than its fellow government sector unions, it has an astonishing asset base of $1.1 billion. Among its assets is a golf course. Thirty-five

UAW executives make more than $150,000, and no fewer than 538 employees make more than $100,000; indeed, the majority of UAW headquarters employees make six-figure salaries (465 make less than $100,000).

Now making a bundle from representing government workers is only half the equation. As well as the cold, hard cash, the union supremos also gain substantial power and influence. In March 2010, President Obama appointed then SEIU President (sorry, *International* President) Andrew Stern to a new commission tasked with coming up with recommendations to help reduce the federal deficit. As my colleague Ivan Osorio noted, Stern's appointment was merely the culmination of a series of appointments by the Obama administration of individuals closely associated with SEIU to government posts. Ivan Osorio reports:

> These include Patrick Gaspard, a former vice president for politics and legislation for SEIU Local 1199, a giant New York health care workers union, who was named White House political director following Obama's election, and SEIU Treasurer Anna Burger, who was named to Obama's Economic Recovery Advisory Board. Then there's former SEIU associate general counsel Craig Becker, whose nomination to the National Labor Relations Board failed in a Senate cloture vote.[7]

Once President Obama moved into the White House, Stern was a frequent guest. According to official visitor logs released in November 2009, Stern visited the White House at least twenty-two times that year (and that was before Christmas party season). That made him the most frequent visitor to the White House during that time (which raises big questions about possible lobbying disclosure violations related to those visits).

That's not to say the SEIU didn't pay heavily for such access. In the 2008 election cycle, the SEIU was the seventh biggest campaign donor.

According to the Center for Responsive Politics, virtually all of its contributions went to Democrats. Stern himself boasted of this spending. He told the *Las Vegas Sun* in May 2009: "We spent a fortune to elect Barack Obama—$60.7 million to be exact—and we're proud of it."

Stern's appointment to the deficit reduction committee was ironic given that government workers, whom he represented, would lose out if the deficit was reduced, which put the interests of Stern and his members in direct conflict with the commission. As Ivan Osorio noted,

> Would Stern be willing to reduce growth of the sector [the taxpayer-supported public sector] where his union is most likely to find new members? More likely are calls for higher taxes to fund more "public services" for SEIU to unionize. That also shouldn't be surprising. Today, government employee unions constitute a permanent special interest lobby favoring the growth of government, one that is motivated, organized and well-funded [by our taxes].

The Myth of the Undercompensated Public Employee

When I started work as a government employee in the United Kingdom, I often found myself, despite my natural frugality, reduced to one meal a day while I waited for my month's end check. I bought in to the belief that government workers should be paid less because they make up for it in better benefits and, in the UK at least, a system of honors that brings prestige to the successful government employee. In the United States, a similar view of a public service ethos used to obtain: you went into the public sector to serve and be rewarded with a generous retirement, while you went into the private sector to earn more but at greater risk. Things have changed dramatically since then. Public sector workers are now paid more than their private sector equivalents by a large, and growing, margin.

USA Today analyzed the data for state and local employees in 2008, and found that public sector workers were "enjoying major gains in compensation, pushing the value of their average wages and benefits far ahead of private workers." In fact, the data from the Bureau of Labor Statistics were unequivocal: "The better pay and benefits for public employees come as private-sector workers face stagnant wages and rising unemployment. State and local government workers now earn an average of $39.50 per hour in total compensation, reports the Bureau of Labor Statistics (BLS). Private workers earn an average of $26.09 an hour."

The *USA Today* survey did not include federal employees. Heritage Foundation labor analyst James Sherk, in his own study, found that federal workers earn 22 percent more per hour than their private-sector counterparts even before taking benefits into account.[8] When benefits are included, the difference rises to 40 percent. Moreover, federal employees enjoy much greater job security—their employment has even *risen* during the recession.

The Cato Institute's Chris Edwards goes further, by comparing average salaries rather than comparable jobs. As far back as 2006, Edwards found that the *average* federal worker earned $100,178 in wages and benefits in 2004, which he compared to $51,876 for the average private sector worker.[9] In other words, the average federal worker earns about *twice as much* in his compensation package as the average private sector worker.

Sherk points out that government pay scales are theoretically based on market-equivalent rates, but these, even if accurately gauged, are negated by the automatic pay rises and frequent promotions that are part and parcel of government work.

As for benefits, one quick look at Sherk's tabulation of federal benefits makes you wonder why anybody would want to work anywhere other than the federal government. The benefits include a premium health insurance plan with no lifetime cap on medical coverage; generous pensions that can be collected by your mid-fifties while you switch over to a new career in the private sector; indulgent paid leave, some of which can be accumulated and cashed out and that can also count to years of service for calculating pension benefits; student loan repayments (up to $60,000); as well as a cornucopia of other benefits. Many federal buildings offer on-site child care. Federal agencies also offer child care subsidies to lower-income federal employees, health care flexible spending accounts, and parking and commuter subsidies. Federal employees may also enroll in federal life insurance, dental, vision, and long-term care insurance plans overseen by the Office of Personnel Management.

Small wonder that private sector workers are about 66 percent more likely to quit their jobs than federal workers are—the feds have it made in the shade; and the public sector unions at the state and local level have used their political muscle, too, to gain extremely generous compensation packages at taxpayers' expense. They succeed because they pay attention to their interests—and so do politicians, who kowtow to the government-employees' union in return for the political support—while taxpayers don't. You have a lot of other things to think about than what bureaucrats in Sacramento or Albany or Washington, D.C., are making. And your public servants take advantage of that by sticking you with a bill for salaries and benefits that most taxpayers could only dream of.

The political class rewards itself with both your tax dollars and political power. For instance, the Hoover Institution's Terry Moe found that teacher's unions

> are quite successful at getting their favored candidates elected to local school boards. When a candidate is supported by the unions, her probability of winning increases dramatically, so much so that the impact of union support appears to be roughly the same as the impact of incumbency. In terms of total impact, union influence may be even greater than this suggests, because union victories literally produce incumbents—and the power of incumbency then works for union candidates to boost their probability of victory still further in future elections.

He also found that "public bureaucrats' [voter] turnout advantage over other citizens is much greater than the existing literature would lead us to expect. It also offers persuasive new grounds for believing that their high turnout is indeed motivated by occupational self-interest—and more generally, that they are actively and purposely engaged in an electoral effort to control their own superiors."[10]

That last sentence is crucial. Unionization of public employees has destroyed the discipline of management. Moe concludes that unionized public employees have more power than the average citizen realizes:

> The prevailing theories treat bureaucrats as mere subordinates, controlled from above by political authorities. But the control relationship can run both ways, and not just because bureaucrats have expertise and other sources of private information. In a democratic system the authorities are elected, and this gives bureaucrats an opportunity to exercise electoral power in determining who will occupy positions of authority and what choices they will make in office. It would be odd indeed if public bureaucrats and their unions did not invest in this kind of reverse control—and there is ample evidence that they do.

No less a figure than Franklin Roosevelt realized that this was a real danger. Government employees were deliberately excluded from his National Labor Relations Act of 1935. FDR explained his reasoning in a letter to the president of the National Federation of Federal Employees in 1937:

> Meticulous attention should be paid to the special relationships and obligations of public servants to the public itself and to the government. All Government employees should realize that the process of collective bargaining, as usually

understood, cannot be transplanted into the public service. It has its distinct and insurmountable limitations.... The very nature and purposes of Government make it impossible for ... officials ... to bind the employer .... The employer is the whole people, who speak by means of laws enacted by their representatives....

Particularly, I want to emphasize my conviction that militant tactics have no place in the functions of any organization of government employees. Upon employees in the federal service rests the obligation to serve the whole people.... This obligation is paramount.... A strike of public employees manifests nothing less than an intent ... to prevent or obstruct ... Government.... Such action, looking toward the paralysis of Government ... is unthinkable and intolerable.

This dam didn't break until 1958, when New York City mayor Robert Wagner, in an effort to ensure his reelection, signed an executive order that allowed city workers to unionize. Government employees rapidly unionized and gained political clout, and accessory politicians mortgaged the taxpayers' future for the public employees' benefit. As former Minnesota governor Tim Pawlenty said in 2010, "Decades of overpromising and fiscal malpractice by state and local officials have created unfunded public employee benefit liabilities of more than $3 trillion."[11]

Governor Pawlenty was able to do the unthinkable. In the state of Walter Mondale and Norm Coleman, he took on the public sector unions over benefits and came out on top:

Public employee unions fought us virtually every step of the way. Mass transit employees, for example, went on strike for 44 days in 2005—because we refused to grant them lifetime health-care benefits after working just 15 years. It was a tough fight, but in the end Minnesota taxpayers won.

We reworked benefits for new hires. We required existing employees to contribute more to their pensions. We reformed our public employee health plan and froze wages.

We proved that even in deep-blue Minnesota, taxpayers can take on big government and big labor, and win.

Several states are following Minnesota's lead, most notably next-door Wisconsin. But whatever gains can be made at the state level, reforming the federal government is going to be much harder. Consider, for instance, the much-ballyhooed federal "pay freeze" touted by President Obama.

The Pay Freeze That Wasn't

In December 2010, President Obama, in an apparent effort to show that he was serious about the nation's fiscal problems, announced that he was freezing the pay of federal workers. Government union leaders erupted in anger. AFGE President John Gage decried the "scapegoating" of federal employees and called it "a superficial, panicked reaction to the deficit commission report." AFL-CIO President Richard Trumka called the freeze "bad for the middle class, bad for the economy and bad for business."

This was all theater, for our benefit. Remember that Andrew Stern sat on the deficit commission. He, Gage, Trumka, and in all likelihood Obama himself knew that any federal pay freeze would have little effect on union members. All it does is stop the automatic annual Cost of Living Adjustment (COLA) raises; federal workers are still likely to get raises based on either criterion.

As reporter F. Vincent Vernuccio explained:

[A]n official at the Office of Management and Budget told Federal News Radio, "employees will still be eligible for step increases."

Step promotions—also known as "within-grade increases"—are mandated by statute. They are nearly automatic as long as an employee performs his job adequately. The law governing federal employee pay states, "a within-grade increase shall be effective on the first day of the first pay period following completion of the required waiting period and in compliance with the conditions of eligibility."

Here's how the system works. Over 70 percent of the federal workforce (except for the military and postal workers) is paid according to the Office of Personnel Management's (OPM) General Schedule (GS) pay scale. GS includes 15 wage grades that reflect the category and skill necessary to perform a job, with 10 steps within each grade.

According to OPM, new employees can expect to receive a step increase every year, mid-level employees every two years, and senior employees every three years. Step increases can range from $728.00 for a GS 3 to $3,321.00 for a GS 15. Grade increases can range from $2,214.00 for a GS 1 to GS 2 to $14,931.00 for a GS 14 to GS 15. These numbers represent the "base" amount for federal pay. The government gives a percentage increase for different areas of the country to reflect local variations in cost of living.

For example, despite the pay freeze, a government employee living in Washington, D.C., who is classified as a GS 14 Step 1 and is upgraded to a GS 15 Step 2, will receive a raise of $22,672. The next year that same federal employee— without a promotion or grade increase—can see their pay go up by $4,126 through a step increase.[12]

Some freeze! In fact, there would have been no COLA increase anyway, because prices had remained static since 2008 (thanks to the recession). This system of automatic pay increases is one reason why top-level government workers are so much better paid today than they were just a few years ago. In fact, since the financial crisis, the number of government workers earning more than $100,000 has exploded. A *USA Today* survey of top government salaries in 2009 found this remarkable statistic: "When the recession started, the Transportation Department had only one person earning a salary of $170,000 or more. Eighteen months later, 1,690 employees had salaries above $170,000."[13]

So, in short, as the economy suffers, federal employees still get richer.

The Defense Department was even worse. In December 2007, there were 1,868 people earning more than $150,000. Less than two years later, in June 2009, there were 10,100 taking home more than that figure. Overall, according to the newspaper's analysis, the number of civil servants getting paid more than $100,000 had increased by a staggering 46 percent to 382,758 between 2007 and 2009. According to the Office of Personnel Management, there are about 2 million federal workers, which means that about one in every five federal employees is making over $100,000.

The rate of pay increase for the most senior workers was even greater. Between 2007 and 2009, the number of federal workers making over $150,000 increased by 119 percent, and the number earning more than $170,000 increased by 93 percent. All this occurred at a time when private sector companies were cutting back wages, salaries, benefits, and jobs in order to stay in business. But in 2008 and 2009 federal employees got across-the-board—congressionally approved—pay raises. (President Obama also asked for an across-the-board federal pay raise in January 2010, eleven months before he announced his meaningless COLA freeze.) In addition, most federal employees got raises for sticking around for another year, and the bureaucracy took advantage of the new system of merit raises to reward itself for having so many meritorious employees. Moreover, whenever the head of an agency gets a raise, a lot of his agency fellows (otherwise salary-capped by what their boss makes) get one too.

Small wonder that the federal pay freeze had no effect whatsoever. That's a bit like what happens when anyone tries to get a government sector worker disciplined or fired.

I Am Not a Slave

When I worked for the British Department of Transport, I had a colleague who always looked harassed when he had to do his annual reports on his staff. It was his bad luck to have a particularly difficult employee. This individual had a stock response whenever his boss asked him to do something: "I am not a slave." True, but this misses the point of paid employment somewhat. My colleague knew that his employee would contest any line in his report that suggested his performance was below par, using every trick in the book to do so, up to and including allegations of discrimination. In the end, he gave the employee a good performance grade, in the hope that he'd get promoted or otherwise move on to a "better" placement within the Department. This was actually quite common. Rather than resort to complex and often interminable disciplinary action, managers would try to get their underperforming employees "kicked upstairs" by means of promotion, so that their problem would become someone else's problem.

It's the same story in America. It is often well-nigh impossible to get a federal, state, or local government employee dismissed, even after egregious behavior. That's because government workers are protected by an array of federal, state, and local laws, appeals procedures, union contracts, and other bureaucratic barriers. This array of protections means that disciplinary procedures are complex, costly, time-consuming, and generally not considered worth the effort. We've all heard the stories of the civil servant who regularly turned up to work drunk (or who actually was regularly drunk and rarely turned up for work) and who was fired only to sue for reinstatement (which he got, along with his lawyer's fees);[14] or the one about the state worker in Arizona that we mentioned back in chapter two. But have you heard the story of Dale Hausner? He murdered six people and yet still had a wrongful dismissal case with the state right up until a month after he was sentenced to death. The Goldwater Institute's Mark Flatten recounts that:

As Dale Hausner was cruising the Valley's streets gunning down innocent victims, he was also getting mediocre performance reviews as a City of Phoenix employee at Sky Harbor International Airport.

Hausner was fired from his job as a custodian at the airport on August 4, 2006, the day after he was arrested as the prime suspect in the Serial Shooter murder spree in which he and a cohort killed at least six people and wounded 19 others during a 14-month reign of terror.

He appealed his dismissal, invoking his rights under a litany of personnel rules and procedures that protect city workers from being disciplined too harshly or too quickly. Though Hausner was not drawing a paycheck as he sat in jail awaiting trial, his appeal to the city's Civil Service Board remained active for the next three years. It finally ended when the appeal was withdrawn in April 2009, a month after he was convicted of first-degree murder and sentenced to death.[15]

Janet Smith, the city's personnel director, explained that the case lingered for so long because the labor union that represents Phoenix's non-emergency government workers, the American Federation of State, County and Municipal Employees, refused to allow Hausner's appeal to be dismissed.

Pension Pain

While public employees may be hard to get rid of when they are employed, they also stay around for a long time after retirement. Public employees have for the most part exceptionally generous pension plans, almost always with defined benefits. In other words, they do not depend for their payout on what the retiree contributes during his career; in many cases the employee contributes nothing at all.

Note also that public employee pension plans—not just for federal workers, but for state and local workers—tend to vest early, meaning that an employee can retire quite early on full pension, say at age fifty, and then proceed to work full-time at another job, earning a full salary, while receiving continuing payments from his former government employer (the taxpayer). The thing is that having to fund a defined-benefit pension scheme for large numbers of employees is a huge liability. With state- and local-government budgets under increasing financial strain, the dangers of legally entrenched benefits to an overpaid special interest have become impossible to ignore. Cities around the country are feeling the pinch.

Vallejo, California, for example, was forced into bankruptcy in 2008 after all other efforts to control costs proved futile. The city spent two years trying to negotiate pay and benefit cuts with its police and fire-fighter unions. Those two departments made up 74 percent of the city's $80 million budget. The unions refused to contemplate any changes, arguing that cuts would compromise public safety. And their generous compensation packages came with a built-in political defense mechanism: Vallejo's 100 firefighters were paying $230 in dues a month, and its 140 police officers $254 a month—which means that the city was paying almost three-quarters of a million dollars each year to fund the war chest with which the unions fought budget cuts. (We'll have more on Vallejo later.)

The problem is not just unsustainable budgets, salaries, and benefits; it is the enormous liabilities in severely underfunded public employee pensions. In early October, Northwestern University's Kellogg School of Management showed that America's fifty largest cities have combined pension underfunding of $574 billion. This is in addition to the liabilities already owed by the states, estimated at between $1 trillion and $3 trillion by various analysts. The taxpayers, of course, have to pay for it all.

But despite this dire situation, America's "public servants" haven't been very public spirited at all. "Greedy" is more like it, clinging to benefits that the state or local government can't afford and wanting to continue gouging the poor taxpayer who likely has no comparable benefits himself.

Which brings us back to Wisconsin: in February 2011, the state Capitol was placed under siege by labor unions. Thousands turned out to protest newly elected Governor Scott Walker's emergency budget bill, which would require teachers to pay more toward their own pensions and limit collective bargaining. Protesters marched through the halls of the Capitol yelling and banging drums. State workers staged a series of demonstrations. Teachers cynically exploited their sick leave allowances and staged a "sickout" strike, claiming illness *en masse* and closing the schools (the education of students apparently being less important to them than padding their pensions with tax dollars and denying themselves the right of deciding whether they wanted to join a union).

Wisconsin is expecting a $3.6 billion deficit over 2011 and 2012. That's a large part of the reason why the state's voters ousted big-spending Democrats in the 2010 election cycle. With government spending under threat, the unions have decided to overturn the democratic process. Governor Walker and other Republicans had campaigned on the manifest need for lower taxes, less government spending, and limits to the power of public employee unions. The unions knew this was coming. Governor Walker told the Associated Press the actions are "not a shock....The shock would be if we didn't go forward with this."[16]

The response from Wisconsin's government unions was loud and clear: Democracy be damned! What good is the will of the people if it takes away union privileges?

Those privileges were indeed extensive. Wisconsin public employees pay nothing into their pensions—try finding a bargain like that in the private sector. The proposed budget will require government employees to contribute 5.8 percent of their pay to their pensions and pick up 12.6 percent of their health care costs. The amounts are roughly half of what private-sector workers pay.

As already noted, the emergency bill also gave workers more protection against forced union membership and dues collection. Unions were incensed because workers would now have a choice and would have to pay affirmatively for union representation.

It is important to note that the bill did not take away the right of workers to join a union. It did not take away their right to bargain collectively—although it did limit such bargaining to wages. It did not force Governor Walker to lay off 6,000 state employees—the amount needed to fix the budget hole. It did not take away other civil-service protections. All it did was bring some fiscal sanity to state pension funding and give employees greater choice over whether to join a union. Yet that was enough for the unions to stage what amounted to an attempted coup d'etat.

Across the country, similar trouble is brewing. In Idaho, similar plans to curtail teachers unions' collective-bargaining powers have led to threats and vandalism directed at the state's schools superintendent. In Ohio, attempts to change the collective-bargaining agreements for police, firefighters, and the highway patrol have led to clashes at the statehouse. Three thousand union activists protesting a bill aimed at restricting public sector collective bargaining confronted tea party activists supporting the bill in the statehouse's rotunda, each side trying to drown the other out.[17] In Tennessee, an attempt to ban teachers' collective bargaining likewise threatened to escalate before Republican lawmakers stepped back and compromised, allowing teachers to bargain locally on salaries and fringe benefits, but not on performance bonuses or assignments.[18] In Indiana, Democrat lawmakers fled the state just like their comrades in Wisconsin to avoid a vote on right-to-work legislation. In their case, however, they managed to force concessions from Republicans before returning. (Without the strong support of Governor Mitch Daniels, who regarded the proposals as a distraction from his focus on education reform, it appears the legislature's Republicans showed their cards too early.)

In all these cases, the struggle pits newly elected representatives and executives against entrenched union power. The unions have powerful allies in Washington, including President Obama, who once noted that "elections have consequences," and in Wisconsin de facto likened those consequences to violence, saying, "Some of what I've heard coming out of Wisconsin, where you're just making it harder for public employees to collectively bargain generally seems like more of an assault on unions." His campaign group, Organizing for America, boasted in February that it was "mobilizing on the ground in Wisconsin."

We should never fool ourselves into thinking that government-sector unions have the best interest of their members in mind when they launch these actions. They are purely and simply directed at maintaining union power and privilege. This was amply demonstrated when the Wisconsin unions offered a series of disingenuous "concessions" to Governor Walker. They offered to have their members pay what the governor demanded for pensions and health care, but did not budge on the issue of forced union dues or collective bargaining. Governor Walker wanted to free teachers from having to pay protection money to the union (and incidentally recoup some of the money they would now have to contribute to their pension and health care benefits). Not surprisingly, what really mattered to the union was keeping the squeeze on their members.

The Wisconsin union gambit was similar to one that our newest public sector union, the Union of Auto Workers, had pulled in Indiana. Under the General Motors bankruptcy proceedings, a shell company called the General Motors Liquidation Company was set up to sell former GM assets to the new, government-owned GM. Some assets, however, were surplus to the government's requirements. Among them was the Indianapolis Metal Center, a plant that produced fenders, hoods, and so on for GM cars and which employed 650 people. Governor Mitch Daniels was very keen to see the plant and jobs saved, and helped to arrange an offer for the plant from J.D. Norman Associates, a local Indiana company, which had plans to supply other automakers as well as GM.

One of the conditions of the Norman offer, however, was that the plant's UAW workers bring their pay closer to the industry average. The result would be roughly a 50 percent pay reduction (to $15.50 an hour). Employees who continued working at the plant and agreed to the reduced salary would retain GM seniority and receive a cash bonus up to $35,000. Employees who did not want to accept the pay cut would be free to transfer to other GM plants for up to two years.

This proved too much for the UAW to accept. Rather than reduce pay and keep the jobs, the UAW preferred to see the plant close, thus losing the jobs to Indianapolis forever. The prospective new owners were mystified. In an open letter to the union on August 17, 2010, Mr. Norman asked the obvious question: "While I understand the sentiment of those employees who would rather transfer to another GM plant, our proposal would guarantee their GM transfer rights without having to close a facility. Why then would any employees want to see the plant close?"

F. Vincent Vernuccio summed up the bullheadedness of the union in a column for Townhall.com:

> The actions of UAW Local 23 illustrate how unions helped bring Detroit automakers to their knees. Members of the local could have simply walked away, moved to other plants and been paid the same amount. They also could have stayed and accepted pay cuts with a bonus. Either option would have allowed a factory to remain open. But that wouldn't have allowed for displays of bravado like that of UAW Local 23 bargaining chairman Gregory Clark, who told the *Indianapolis Star*, "The contract they offered us wasn't a contract....It just gutted everything we had come to know as a contract between employers and employees."
>
> So the union chose to close the plant. Most members of the local will now be allowed to transfer to other facilities

anyway, but the toll on the local economy will linger. The plant pays $1.8 million a year to Marion County in property taxes and has a payroll of about $40 million. The potential workers who would have been hired had the plant remained open will now have a harder time finding new jobs.[19]

This is exactly the sort of attitude on display in Wisconsin and other states. Union powers and privileges are the be-all and end-all of public sector employment. No other considerations—especially not the public good—come into play.

PART FOUR

YOUR FRIENDLY LOCAL ROBBER BARONS

CHAPTER EIGHT

MUNICIPAL MADNESS

Between the passage of the American Recovery and Reinvestment Act (the "stimulus act") in February 2009 and March 31, 2010, the city of Los Angeles received over half a billion dollars in stimulus funds from the federal government. Of that, $111 million went to two city departments: Public Works and Transportation. Between them, according to reports by City Controller Wendy Greuel, the departments managed to use that money to "save or create" just fifty-five jobs (at about $2 million per job), nearly all of them, apparently, in the public sector. The number of created private sector jobs appears to be so small that it could be counted on the fingers of one hand. That's what happens when you give local bureaucrats the opportunity to spend $111 million. For the most part, they spend it on themselves. During that time, unemployment in Los Angeles rose above 12 percent.

California's State Controller John Chiang has been a perfect example of an intransigent bureaucrat shielding public sector workers from economic reality. In 2008, then-Governor Arnold Schwarzenegger ordered Chiang to cut the salaries of 200,000 state employees to the federal minimum wage to help close a gaping budget gap. Chiang refused to do so. First he claimed he had a constitutional right to refuse the order. Then he said the outdated computer paycheck system couldn't handle the change. The judiciary decided that the first argument had no merit, but agreed with him on the second, saying that computer issues were not trivial.

A few days after John Chiang won his victory over the Governator thanks to his old computer system, he issued a statement saying that the state was unable to pay $15.6 billion worth of bills.[1] In other words, under Chiang's computer system, if you were a state employee, you got paid; if you were a private individual owed money from the state—tough luck.

Chiang's three-year campaign of intransigence paid off. In 2010, Californians elected Democrat Jerry Brown governor, and Brown quickly dropped a lawsuit, left over from the Schwarzenegger administration, asserting the governor's right to impose minimum wage-level payments on state employees during a budget crisis.

Not surprisingly, Chiang is a favorite of government sector unions. The Service Employees International Union (SEIU) has maxed out its contributions to Chiang's campaigns every year since he has been in office, according to Meredith Turney of the activist group Americans for Prosperity. Chiang received more than $190,000 in campaign contributions from state employee labor unions in his 2010 re-election bid, which accounted for nearly 22 percent of all his contributions. According to campaign reports filed through May 22, 2010, Chiang received large donations from the California Teachers Association, SEIU, Electrical Workers Union, Firefighters Union, California Labor Federation Operating Engineers, and the California State Council of Service Employees.

If government employees can expect to be paid in full however bad the state's budget crisis, it should be no surprise that they have other legal protections as well. Former *Orange County Register* reporter Steven Greenhut, author of the must-read book *Plunder! How Public Employee*

Unions Are Raiding Treasuries, Controlling Our Lives and Bankrupting the Nation, revealed how massive numbers of California state employees are free to run red lights and commit other driving offenses in an article for *Reason* magazine in 2010:

> Drivers of nearly 1 million cars and light trucks—out of a total 22 million vehicles registered statewide—were protected by a "shield" in the state records system between their license plate numbers and their home addresses. There were, the newspaper found, great practical benefits to this secrecy.
>
> "Vehicles with protected license plates can run through dozens of intersections controlled by red light cameras with impunity," the [Orange County] *Register*'s Jennifer Muir reported. "Parking citations issued to vehicles with protected plates are often dismissed because the process necessary to pierce the shield is too cumbersome. Some patrol officers let drivers with protected plates off with a warning because the plates signal that drivers are 'one of their own' or related to someone who is."

Like most programs that you'll find like this, the program started out with good intentions:

> The plate program started in 1978 with the seemingly unobjectionable purpose of protecting the personal addresses of officials who deal directly with criminals. Police argued that the bad guys could call the Department of Motor Vehicles (DMV), get addresses for officers, and use the information to harm them or their family members. There was no rash of such incidents, only the possibility that they could take place.
>
> So police and their families were granted confidentiality. Then the program expanded from one set of government workers to another. Eventually parole officers, retired parking

enforcers, DMV desk clerks, county supervisors, social workers, and other categories of employees from 1,800 state agencies were given the special protections too.

Even as the program was expanding, its initial rationale ceased to exist.
The DMV stopped giving out *anyone's* name and address. Problem
solved, simply and inexpensively; but the program kept on growing. You
would expect that, after the *Orange County Register* revealed the program's needless existence, it would be abolished without any fuss. You'd
be wrong. As Greenhut reveals, the opposite happened:

> Here is how brazen they've become: A few days after the
> newspaper investigation caused a buzz in Sacramento, law-
> makers voted to *expand* the driver record protections to even
> more government employees. An Assembly committee, on a
> bipartisan 13-to-0 vote, agreed to extend the program to
> veterinarians, firefighters, and code officers. "I don't want to
> say no to the firefighters and veterinarians that are doing these
> things that need to be protected," Republican Assemblyman
> Mike Duvall of Yorba Linda explained.[2]

So much for equal protection of the laws. Remember this: government
always looks after its own, not the taxpayers who get stuck with the check.

Local Taxes, Local Benefits

When I had my first child and came to fill in my tax form the next
year, I noticed an oddly compassionate note regarding the child tax exemption. It said something along the lines of "If your child lived, even for just
a short time, during the tax year, you may claim the entire exemption."
This struck me as remarkably sympathetic for the IRS, even if it was probably motivated by the fear of bad publicity for coming after someone for
an extra day's taxes when their child died early on New Year's Eve.

However, even as the feds leave people alone in their grief, some local and municipal governments are ready to charge a few dollars more.

Take King County, Washington, for example. The Clark family, from Yakima, traveled to the University of Washington Medical Center in Seattle, which is located in King County, for the birth of their daughter Olivia. Little Olivia was born without any lungs, and it is a miracle that she was able to survive for an hour after birth. "We were thrilled that she lived long enough that we could meet her alive and talk about her and see her while she was still alive," said Larry Clark, her grandfather.[3]

After the funeral, the Kings were amazed to see a small line item on their bill, reading "King County death tax: $50." King County, it transpired, requires a review of every death, with the fee attached to the bill for cremation or burial. Gareth Johnson, King County "Prevention Division" Manager, told Channel 5 news, "The reason we do that is to make sure no one goes to the crematorium or to their grave without society and the family knowing exactly how their loved one died."

That may in some cases be justified, but for a little girl born without lungs who died with her family and doctors surrounding her, one might think the requirement a tad unnecessary. Larry Clark spoke for many when he said, "Every time I turn around the county appears to be nickel-and-diming us, putting a tax on this and a tax on that. Where does it end?"

No end is in sight, apparently. While King County was the only one in the state to require a review of every death (with a fee, of course), a King County Public Health spokesman was proud to say that other counties and jurisdictions were "shifting towards the process."

When they're not nickel-and-diming you to distraction, there are many local and municipal governments happily spending your money on bizarre benefits for their employees. Take good old Berkeley, California. In January 2011, at a time when other municipalities were facing economic reality and trying to restrict employee benefits, Berkeley City Council thought it would be a good idea to add one. The proposal, which was supposed to be voted on in February 2011 but was not, would set aside $20,000 annually of taxpayer money to pay for employees' sex-change operations.[4]

The councilman who first proposed the idea in 2007, Darryl Moore, said, "We offer all kinds of benefits to our employees. This brings our benefits in line with what's just and fair for the transgender community." Even residents of famously liberal Berkeley were more worried about what was just and fair to them. A former zoning commissioner said, "How come I'm paying for this? There might be some people who really need this, but right now my street badly needs paving." At the same time the Berkeley City Council was considering the proposal, it was in the middle of a hiring freeze and was facing an unfunded pension liability of $252 million.

While we're in California, let's take a trip to Vista. This city, just to the north of San Diego, is home to about 100,000 people. It has also run up a huge budget deficit (stop me if you've heard this one) and needed to cut about $9 million from its 2011 operating budget. Rather than find cuts to non-essential staff and services from, for instance, its $10.5 billion "general government" budget or its $8.5 million budget for "culture and recreation," including management of the Wave Waterpark, it decided to stop providing an essential service instead, threatening to turn off the lights: "To trim $9 million from their budget, Vista officials say they will shut off half of the city's residential street lights in March unless property owners agree to pay higher lighting fees. Fees could cost residents of the north San Diego County city between $4 and $20 a year."[5]

Residents were incensed, not just by the blatant extortion, but also by the fact that Vista City Hall's lights kept blazing. The city spokesperson responded, cool as a cucumber:

> City spokeswoman Andrea McCullough tells the North County Times that lights in the park behind the building have been shut off and lights in front of the Civic Center have been dimmed. Inside the building, she says lights are being dimmed

at 7 p.m. instead of 10 p.m. Most lights are energy-efficient so dimming them won't save much, but McCullough says residents will at least know the city is doing its part.

As is widely known, street lighting is an important defense against crime (more effective, in fact, than Big Brother's beloved closed circuit TV). Vista's government made a conscious decision to put its own citizens in danger rather than reduce its budget in a responsible fashion. In any government budget crisis, you will always see the same reaction—government looks after its own and looks to punish the taxpayer: so the first things on the chopping block are what taxpayers value (like public safety) rather than limiting the perks and special interest programs of the entrenched bureaucracy.

Bellwether

Perhaps the most incredible story of municipal misuse of taxpayer funds comes from the Los Angeles suburb of Bell, California. In July 2010, Bell residents were astonished to read a series of *Los Angeles Times* investigations exposing top city officials siphoning vast sums of taxpayer money into personal bank accounts:

> Bell, one of the poorest cities in Los Angeles County, pays its top officials some of the highest salaries in the nation, including nearly $800,000 annually for its city manager, according to documents reviewed by *The Times*.
>
> In addition to the $787,637 salary of Chief Administrative Officer Robert Rizzo, Bell pays Police Chief Randy Adams $457,000 a year, about 50% more than Los Angeles Police Chief Charlie Beck or Los Angeles County Sheriff Lee Baca and more than double New York City's police commissioner. Assistant City Manager Angela Spaccia makes $376,288 annually, more than most city managers.

Top officials have routinely received hefty annual raises in recent years. Rizzo's contract calls for 12% raises each July, the same as his top deputy, according to documents obtained under the California Public Records Act.[6]

Perhaps almost as offensive as these massive salaries was the reaction of Robert Rizzo, who had been City Manager for almost twenty years, and his colleagues to the news being made public:

> "If that's a number people choke on, maybe I'm in the wrong business," he said. "I could go into private business and make that money. This council has compensated me for the job I've done."
>
> Spaccia agreed, adding: "I would have to argue you get what you pay for."
>
> Bell Mayor Oscar Hernandez defended the salaries. "Our city is one of the best in the area. That is the result of the city manager. It's not because I say it. It's because my community says it."

That excuse didn't wash with the experts the *Times* interviewed:

> Experts in city government said they were amazed at the salaries the city pays, particularly Rizzo's. "I have not heard anything close to that number in terms of compensation or salary," said Dave Mora, West Coast regional director of the International City/County Management Assn., and a retired city manager.
>
> By comparison, Manhattan Beach, a far wealthier city with about 7,000 fewer people, paid its most recent city manager $257,484 a year. The city manager of Long Beach, with a population close to 500,000, earns $235,000 annually. Los Angeles County Chief Executive William T. Fujioka makes $338,458.

Given that one in six of the city's residents lives in poverty, the news of the inflated salaries and other payments had them marching in the streets in protest:

> Several hundred angry residents from a modest blue-collar Los Angeles suburb marched Sunday to call for the resignation of the mayor and some City Council members in a protest sparked by the sky-high salaries of three recently departed administrators.
>
> The residents of the city of Bell marched to Oscar's Korner Market and Carniceria, owned by Mayor Oscar Hernandez, then to his home, demanding that he reduce his own six-figure compensation or quit.
>
> They then did the same with some members of the City Council, with many marchers wearing T-shirts that read "My city is more corrupt than your city."[7]

Further investigation by the *Times* revealed that the situation was worse than they thought, once the officials' benefit packages were taken into account:

> The *Times* reviewed Rizzo's benefits package for this year, which covers time off, retirement and medical and other types of insurance. The package entitled him to vacation and sick leave that totaled more than 28 weeks a year....
>
> The newly reviewed records show that when the benefits package is added, Assistant City Manager Angela Spaccia's $376,288 salary more than doubles to $845,960. Police Chief Randy Adams' pay jumps from $457,000 to $770,046 annually.
>
> Spaccia was to have received $188,640 in vacation and sick pay and Adams $76,428, the records show. Adams, according to his contract, was to have received lifetime medical benefits for him and his family.[8]

Further revelations included the fact that Rizzo wrote his own retirement plan, which guaranteed that he would receive a million dollars a year within a few years.

More investigations revealed some irregularities surrounding the pay arrangements for police Chief Randy Adams. He had been declared disabled the day after his hiring, which means that he gets half his pension tax free under California law. His disability, however, did not stop him from competing in a 5K run or from claiming how much he liked to ski in a job application to Orange County. Emails later released by prosecutors suggest that Adams might have had an inkling of what was going on in Bell:

> As Bell prepared to hire a police chief in 2009, the top candidate for the post exchanged e-mails with the city's No. 2 official: "I am looking forward to seeing you and taking all of Bell's money?!" Randy Adams wrote shortly before starting the job. "Okay...just a share of it!!"
>
> "LOL...well you can take your share of the pie...just like us!!!" responded Angela Spaccia, the city's assistant administrator. "We will all get fat together....Bob has an expression he likes to use on occasion," she continued, referring to her boss and chief administrative officer, Robert Rizzo. "Pigs get Fat...Hogs get slaughtered!!!! So as long as we're not Hogs...All is well!"[9]

Meanwhile, the city council's members (with one exception) were revealed to have been paid about $100,000 annually for meetings that did not occur or lasted only a few minutes.

In September 2010, Robert Rizzo, Mayor Oscar Hernandez, former assistant city manager Angela Spaccia, and council members George Mirabal, Teresa Jacobo, Luis Artiga, George Cole, and Victor Bello were arrested. Rizzo was charged with unjust enrichment, negligence, breach of fiduciary duty, and fraud, among other crimes. Rizzo's pension was reduced to $100,000 a year in December 2010. In January 2011, an audit suggested the city was near bankruptcy. The next week, Hernandez, Jacobo, and Cole claimed in court that the city of Bell should pay their legal expenses.[10]

Death Vallejo

Bell is obviously an extreme example, but a more prosaic example of bad management comes from the city of Vallejo, California, which in 2008 became the first to apply for municipal bankruptcy, because it couldn't pay its unionized employees what it had promised them. The city faced a $16.6 million budget shortfall. Ivan Osorio describes what precipitated the city to declare bankruptcy:

> The city had been negotiating with the police and firefighter unions for about two years. City officials asked for salary, benefit, and staff cuts, but the unions retorted that those would endanger public safety and the safety of the police and firefighters. Police and firefighter salaries, pensions, and over-time accounted for 74 percent of Vallejo's $80-million general budget, significantly higher than the state average of 60 percent. Contracts include minimum staffing requirements, which significantly increased overtime pay. And how generous could contracts get? A police captain, for example, could receive $306,000 a year in pay and benefits, a lieutenant $247,644, with the average for firefighters at $171,000 (with 21 earning over $200,000, including overtime). Police and firefighters become eligible for lifetime health benefits. In 2007, 292 city employees made over $100,000.[11]

The unions contested the bankruptcy, arguing that the city could raise taxes, cut expenses, and raid a $136 million off-budget reserve fund (legally dedicated to state bondholders) to find the money "owed" to the public employees. On September 4, 2008, the city's petition for bankruptcy protection was approved. The police and fire unions appealed the ruling a couple weeks later, but dropped their appeal in August 2009.

Public employee pension liabilities are an albatross around the necks of state and local government, but because they have the status of a legal contract, it is difficult to do anything about them. The result is that taxpayers are on the hook for massive entitlements. The California state employee pension program operates on a "three percent at 50" arrangement, which means that a state employee can retire at fifty with 3 percent of his final salary for every year he's worked for the government. Do the math: someone who started work at age twenty can retire on his fiftieth birthday with 90 percent of his final salary rolling in every year for the rest of his life, even if he takes another job. Nice work—or retirement—if you can get it, and you can get it if you're a state employee. But arrangements like this are killing state finances all over the nation, and they don't look so attractive if you're a taxpayer.

Yet many local authorities aren't so much facing up to the crisis as compounding it. Steven Greenhut gives us a galling example from Fullerton, California.

> The city council in 2009 sought to retroactively increase the defined-benefit retirement plan for its city employees by a jaw-dropping 25 percent. What's more, the Fullerton City Council negotiated the increase in closed session, outside public view. Under California's open meetings law, known as the Brown Act, even legitimate closed-session items such as contract negotiations are supposed to be advertised so that the public has a clear idea of what's being discussed. But the Fullerton agenda for that night only vaguely referred to labor negotiations.
>
> Four of the five council members—two Republicans and two Democrats—seemed to support the deal. But Republican Shawn Nelson, a principled advocate for limited government,

didn't appreciate the way the council was obscuring not only the legitimately secret details of the negotiations but the basic subject matter. He called me at the [*Orange County*] *Register* (where I worked at the time) and, without revealing details of the closed session, shared his concerns about the way the public had not been alerted.[12]

Marxists often talk about class enemies, but what is much worse to them is the class traitor. Greenhut continues:

After I wrote about the secret, fiscally reckless deal, the recriminations came down in a hurry: on Shawn Nelson.

Not surprisingly, the liberal council members were furious that the public had been informed about what was going on. But some conservative Republicans, including a prominent state senator, Dick Ackerman of Irvine, were angry as well, because Nelson's willingness to talk embarrassed a Republican councilman whom the GOP was backing for re-election. When I later bumped into Ackerman at the Republican National Convention in St. Paul, he laid into me about Nelson's supposed violation of the Brown Act. Some officials and bloggers actually called for Nelson to be prosecuted. Local union mouthpieces and fellow council members portrayed the whistleblower as a common criminal, even though he was merely acting in the spirit of the open meetings law and showing the kind of fiscal responsibility you would hope to see in public officials.

In this case, however, transparency worked. Local citizens didn't like the look they had been given at how this pork sausage was made. The city council backed down, finally, but not until Nelson and Greenhut had both suffered public skewering. Greenhut was also accused of libel.

Even when cities are taking steps to reduce public spending, the cuts they make are often forced on them by previous decisions to wall off things like pensions. Take the example of the Orange County Sheriff, Sandra Hutchens, who was forced to cut 40 percent of her command budget, resulting in what she felt were compromises to public safety. Steven Greenhut again:

> The sheriff failed to identify another reason for the tight budget: In 2001 the Orange County Board of Supervisors had passed a retroactive pension increase for sheriff's deputies. That policy nearly doubled pension costs from 2000 to 2009, when pension contributions totaled nearly $95 million—20 percent of the sheriff's budget. So the sheriff decries an economic downturn that is costing her department about $20 million, but she doesn't mention that a previous pension increase is costing her department more than double that amount. It's safe to say that had the pension increase not passed, the department would have money to keep officers on the streets and to avoid the cuts the sheriff claims are threatening public safety.

It's the contractual nature of these arrangements that makes them such an obstacle to genuine reform of public finances. That's why Vallejo's move to bankruptcy protection was so important. It may yet provide the best answer to the mess our state and local robber barons have gotten us into.

A Real Sense of Entitlement

Another major cost to the government you pay for is overtime. New York's Metropolitan Transportation Authority (MTA) is a case in point for just how big the problem is. In 2009, more than 8,000 of its employees made over $100,000, including conductors, police officers, and engineers. Inflated government salaries might not surprise you anymore. But here's the kicker: the *New York Times* noted that many of them made over six figures in overtime and retirement benefits alone.[13]

One retiring conductor, Thomas J. Redmond, managed to make $239,148—more than the MTA's Chief Financial Officer. He and two other Long Island Railroad workers were among the top twenty-five income earners at the MTA. The *Times* detailed how Mr. Redmond and other high-earning rank-and-file workers did it: Mr. Redmond, who was the eighth-highest paid employee, earned $67,772 as a base salary, an additional $67,000 in overtime, and nearly $100,000 in lieu of unused sick and vacation days on his retirement. Another employee, a lieutenant named Walter Stock, took home $226,383, while Dominick J. Masiello, a locomotive engineer on the Long Island Rail Road, earned $75,000 in base salary, overtime worth $52,000, and "penalty payments" of $94,600. These payments derive from contractual agreements that engineers working in storage yards have to be paid extra to move a locomotive to another facility or otherwise operate outside the yard.

In Massachusetts, meanwhile, if you're an Assistant Clerk in the state court system, you live a life of leisure. An investigation by the Boston CBS affiliate found, "There are 441 assistant clerks across the state and if you add up vacation, sick days, personal days and holidays, 223 of them get 76 days, or nearly four months off. Most of the remaining clerks, 146, get 61 days, or slightly more that three months off."[14]

You expect that, with all that time off, they must be low-paid, part-time employees. Think again: they might be part-time, but they're not low-paid. The Boston CBS affiliate reported, "Back in the summer, the I-Team caught one of those assistant court clerks, since-retired Stephen Donovan, taking even more time off on the taxpayers' dime. We recorded Donovan with our hidden cameras taking long lunches at a downtown Boston bar, downing drink after drink while court was in session. Donovan was paid $84,869 a year, which is the salary for most assistant clerks."

Sick leave is also a matter for controversy in Massachusetts. Port Authority (Massport) workers employed before 2007 get to cash in any untaken sick leave up to that point when they retire, often for six-figure payments. When the Massport CEO, Thomas Kinton, retires (he started working at Massport in 1976), that state will be on the hook for at least $455,000 in unpaid sick time. Unused sick time since 2007 can be cashed in for 20 percent of its value. In 2009, the state paid workers $6.3 million for unused sick time.

The Protection Racket

Yet the political robber barons aren't just politicos and bureaucrats. Increasingly, they include the people we trust the most for our protection. Police and fire departments all over the nation have gone from being heroic defenders of our lives to legalized protection rackets, demanding ever-higher taxes. Not surprisingly, massively increased budgets for crime-fighting haven't led to massively decreased crime rates, for reasons you can probably guess by now.

Like most people on the right, I have a tremendous regard for police officers. In some places, they put their lives on the line every day to protect us from the unsavory elements of society, and they deserve good pay and conditions. But what many people don't realize is that police departments (and fire departments) are becoming highly unionized, and in the process, the interests of taxpayers are starting to be sacrificed, in the usual way, to the interests of the public safety bureaucracy. As an example of what I'm talking about, let's look at the Port Authority Police Department in New York. Because of a clause in their union contract, officers can collect overtime payments when they are *not* working. The *New York Post* explains:

> The bizarre benefit applies to officers suspected of misconduct who are suspended with pay and later cleared or found guilty of an infraction carrying a penalty that's short of dismissal.

Suspended officers can claim overtime if no formal charges are filed within 120 days.

The theoretical overtime these cops would have made during their suspensions is based on a formula in their union contract.[15]

So an officer can be found guilty of a disciplinary offense and still get rewarded for work he or she never performed, all based on a union-derived "right" to overtime. It should also be noted that the Port Authority pays $60,000 a year towards the rent for the union's headquarters in New Jersey.

Down in North Carolina, the city of Durham's police chief signed off on thousands of dollars of overtime for one officer despite concerns being raised by managers. Alesha Robinson-Taylor, a twelve-year veteran who handled off-duty jobs for officers, alcohol permits, and towing schedules, managed to secure $59,545 in overtime from October 2008 to July 2009. Her annual salary was just $52,665. Auditors calculated, according to WRAL News, that the officer "would have had to work 79 hours per week, including the 16 weeks she was on leave, to accumulate the amount of overtime she claimed. Time sheets, phone records and e-mail logs couldn't substantiate the amount of overtime, the audit states."[16]

This might seem like a simple case of one officer misbehaving. However, when the officer's superior complained to the deputy police chief who had approved the overtime without documentation, he was reassigned to other duties. And when the concerns were taken to the police chief himself, he said that the claims "did not seem out of line" and that he couldn't take any further action without documentation.

The problem seems even more rife in Boston, Massachusetts. According to the *Boston Globe*, several police captains and lieutenants make over $200,000 and regularly pull in another $30,000 to $50,000 in overtime.[17] Boston police commissioner Ed Davis, who achieved an amazing reduction in crime while serving as police chief in Lowell, Massachusetts, called the salaries "excessive."

When it was revealed that overtime abuses were still going on despite an audit questioning the practice in 2001 (five years before Davis took charge), he launched a probe into the overtime scandal. A particular concern for Davis is "courtroom pay," where officers can earn four hours' worth of overtime for a court appearance outside their shift, even when the court appearance only requires half an hour of their time. Four officers have been placed on leave so far as a result of the probe.

The earlier audit had revealed considerable abuse, with over 400 separate incidents detailed. Captain William Broderick, head of the internal affairs unit, had alleged, "Officers had gotten into certain habits... (and) were doing things, but they were doing things with their supervisors' OK, and the supervisors were doing things with their supervisors' OK." Broderick was fired after making the allegations, and was later awarded $2.8 million by a jury for breach of his civil rights in the firing.[18]

Davis vowed to continue his probe, telling the *Boston Herald*, "I intend to provide the community with a police agency that utilizes its financial support efficiently. The community can remain confident in our efforts to ensure an effective and well-managed police organization as we move forward serving the City of Boston."

If only every police officer was as conscientious as Ed Davis.

Burn, Baby, Burn

Firefighters work long hours—about 2,400 a year, 1,000 more than teachers—and put their lives on the line to save our lives and property (although, statistically, the job is less dangerous than fishing, logging, and many other private sector occupations). Yet even this noble profession, thanks to unionization, has grown contemptuous of the public.

The fact is that 72 percent of America's firefighters are volunteers, not professionals. Many Americans help man the pumps out of a sense of duty, at no cost to their neighbors. That suggests that the high salaries of municipal firefighters are out of touch with the market. That disparity becomes starker when the low rate of fires in urban areas is taken into account. As Steven Greenhut points out in *Plunder!*, 90 percent of urban emergency calls to fire departments are for paramedic services—"services which could be privately provided ... but which have been co-opted by the firefighters as unions have used their legal muscle to drive out most private competitors." The long hours claim is also misleading—firefighters are paid for sleeping (or "while sleeping" as one of Greenhut's correspondents preferred to put it).

Fire departments often claim that they can't afford to upgrade their equipment. This should not be a surprise when so much of their budget goes to salaries. Private and even volunteer sector fire departments tend not to suffer from this problem, so the problem is clearly an artifact of public management and union interference.

Many people know what a sweet deal a fire department job is. They have to hold recruiting events at public auditoriums to accommodate the large number of people wanting to get in on the act. This is in itself a problem. People who don't really want to be firefighters and whose talents are better suited to other occupations will become firefighters because of the compensation, which in turn crowds out those who really want to be firefighters for the duties involved, and who would be better at the job.

Steven Greenhut concludes that in many ways the problems of municipal fire departments are a perfect example of what has gone wrong with local government:

> Throwing public money at things, as always, distorts the market and causes unforeseen problems. Yet these realities never get much public policy discussion. That's another consequence of public union dominance—serious policy issues are off the table if they conflict with the thinking of union leaders.

In Orange County, California, the average total pay and benefits package for a firefighter is worth $175,000 a year. What's yours?

The Californian Disease

According to the *Sacramento Bee*, in one year, 2002, 82 percent of retiring California Highway Patrol (CHP) officers retired on disability terms. Could conditions really be so bad that 82 percent of retiring officers were permanently disabled?

Of course not—the CHP officers had just discovered what in Britain they call a "nice little earner." It's a loophole that allows them workers' compensation on top of their already generous "three percent at 50" retirement arrangements. It's known as "the Californian Disease" because remunerative "disability" is particularly common among public workers in California; indeed, more than two-thirds of CHP management-level employees claim disability shortly before their retirement.

John Hill and Dorothy Korber of the *Sacramento Bee* found that "High-ranking [CHP] officers, nearing the end of their careers, routinely pursued disability claims that awarded them workers' comp settlements. That, in turn, led in many cases to disability retirements. As they collected their disability pensions, some of these former CHP chiefs embarked on rigorous second careers—one as assistant sheriff of Yolo County, for example, another as the security director for San Francisco International Airport."

As the *Bee* noted, the number of such claims spiked when the Department temporarily closed down its fraud investigation unit, which suggests very strongly that these officers knew exactly what they were doing and that it was indeed fraud on a grand scale.

The disease isn't confined to the police force; fire departments are susceptible as well, as are other government organizations across California. The "3 percent at 50" plan led John Derbyshire to comment, "If you did not follow my oft-repeated advice to GET A GOVERNMENT

JOB!, you will still be toiling away at age 75 to finance the Caribbean cruises of 55-year-old public-sector retirees. Thanks, suckers!"[19]

It's hard to decide on the most outrageous case, though the winner might be Mike Clesceri, part-time Mayor of Fullerton, the city that tried to vote through a 25 percent retrospective pension rise in secret. Clesceri worked for the District Attorney's Office in Orange County as investigator. The job apparently gave him heartburn—literally. He claimed to have such a bad case of acid reflux that he had to retire from his DA job with a disability, which entitled him to a pension of $58,000 a year—tax free, plus cost-of-living increases. Clesceri, however, appeared to believe in an active retirement. He kept his job as mayor, tried to become a police chief, ran for re-election, and even had his lawyer threaten to sue anyone who questioned his disability, which, Clesceri said, only affected his job with the District Attorney. Mr. Clesceri, incidentally, is a self-described conservative and a Republican.

But, according to Steven Greenhut, the Democrats are the party that is joined at the hip with the public employees unions. So much so that when the Police Officers Research Association of California, a union lobbying group, interviewed Democrat candidates for Attorney General, they only had two questions, one of which was whether as Attorney General the candidates would ensure that the official ballot summary of an initiative to reform state pensions was written in the most pro-pension way possible. In every case, the candidates answered yes. So much for disinterested public servants. It's a sad day when "to protect and serve" has come to refer to protecting pensions and serving public employee unions. But that's where we are.

CHAPTER NINE

THE EDUCATION BUBBLE

If anything is more sacrosanct than public safety, it's education. It's hard to lose an election promising more money for education and hard to win one if you advocate cutting the education budget. But an astonishing amount of money in public education budgets doesn't go to educators, it goes to turf-protecting bureaucrats who ensure that whenever the education budget comes under scrutiny, it's always the libraries put under threat, not the central offices.

The educators themselves aren't doing too badly. Contrary to urban legend, they are well-paid with great benefits. Tenured professors at state schools have it even better, big salaries, light workloads, and no danger of being fired. Moreover, our public universities have used publicly financed student loans to jack up tuition fees. The irony is that a college degree is worth less and less even as universities rake in more and more.

A Lesson on
School Teacher Salaries

First we should dismiss the popular myth that teachers are underpaid. Former First Lady Laura Bush fell for this one when her husband was in office. "Salaries are too low. We all know that," she said, before asserting, "We need to figure out a way to pay teachers more."[1] We often hear arguments like that of Ron Clark, a teaching expert and author, who told CNN, "Teacher pay is so low it's ridiculous. When I was in college, I had a lot of friends who wanted to be teachers, but they decided not to, because they needed to support a family." Clark wants teachers paid an annual salary of $100,000.[2] *Washington Post* columnist Richard Cohen wants teachers exempted from income tax.[3]

Let's look at teacher salaries around the nation. According to the National Center for Education Statistics, the average salary for public school teachers in 2008–2009 was $53,910. How you compute whether teachers are underpaid or overpaid depends on how you crunch the numbers. Even the American Federation of Teachers (AFT) conceded that "teachers earned the same, on average, as other government employees in 2007," though this represented lost ground because ten years earlier they were earning 7 percent more. But, of course, the AFT is all in favor of higher salaries for public employees in general and teachers in particular, and claimed that the "average employee in one of the 23 professions the Bureau of Labor Statistics (BLS) deems comparable to teachers in terms of education/training requirements made on average $72,678 in 2007, compared with the $51,009 earned by a teacher."[4]

But these calculations cook the books. Jay Greene and Marcus Winters of the Manhattan Institute also used Bureau of Labor Statistics (BLS) data but broke it down in terms of hourly wage, and this reveals a very different conclusion:

> According to the BLS, the average public school teacher in the
> United States earned $34.06 per hour in 2005.... The average

white-collar worker (excluding sales [whose earnings are often based on commissions]) earned $25.08 per hour, and the average professional specialty and technical worker earned $30.66 per hour. The average public school teacher was paid 36% more per hour than the average non-sales white-collar worker and 11% more than the average professional specialty and technical worker. Nationwide, public school teachers earn more than the [comparable] average workers.[5]

Greene and Winters found that the highest paid teachers were in Detroit ($47.28 per hour), San Francisco ($46.70), and New York ($45.79), but when comparing earnings to similar groups, the highest relative salaries came in Elkhart, Indiana (87 percent more than the average white collar worker), Grand Rapids, Michigan (80 percent more), and Louisville, Kentucky (79 percent more). Detroit teachers still ranked high, in eighth place, earning 61 percent more than white collar workers.

Among other important findings, Greene and Winters discovered:

- Full-time public school teachers work on average 36.5 hours per week during weeks that they are working. By comparison, white-collar workers (excluding sales) work 39.4 hours, and professional specialty and technical workers work 39.0 hours per week. Private school teachers work 38.3 hours per week.
- Compared with public school teachers, editors and reporters earn 24% less; architects, 11% less; psychologists, 9% less; chemists, 5% less; mechanical engineers, 6% less; and economists, 1% less.
- Compared with public school teachers, airplane pilots earn 186% more; physicians, 80% more; lawyers, 49% more; nuclear engineers, 17% more; actuaries, 9% more; and physicists, 3% more.

- Public school teachers are paid 61% more per hour than private school teachers, on average nationwide.

As part of their analysis, Greene and Winters also looked at whether teachers who were paid relatively higher than similar occupations in their area produced demonstrably higher graduation rates. They did not. Nor, for that matter, did per-pupil spending or the student-teacher ratio affect graduation rates. What did increase graduation rates was having more small school districts in a metro area, which strongly suggests that school choice increases competition for students and the revenue that comes with them, which in turn improves performance.

The teachers' lobby always claims that teachers regularly work after hours, but Greene and Winters dealt with this objection in a *Wall Street Journal* piece about their research, contending that the National Compensation Survey already takes all hours worked into account, and that other occupations regularly work overtime as well. Indeed, given that "mandatory unpaid overtime" is a phenomenon most seen in the private sector, if anything the comparable private sector occupations suffer more in this regard, rather than less.[6]

There's also the matter of teachers' deferred compensation to consider. As Joel Klein, former Chancellor of New York City's public schools, has pointed out, teachers' pension schemes actually hurt public education and therefore our children.[7]

For a start, most jurisdictions have systematically underfunded pension schemes for years (doesn't that sound familiar?), so now that the liabilities have caught up with the lack of assets to cover them, education authorities are having to divert funds from education to pay long-retired teachers' pensions. The problem is likely to get much worse before it gets anywhere near better, as there are many teachers in the system now who will get the same terms when they retire.

It's not just that, however. The way teacher benefits are packaged, they create odd incentives that end up with our children having worse teachers. For instance, because of the generous terms at retirement, most teacher compensation packages are weighted heavily away from the beginning of the career. So even counting the generous vacation allowances, the needs of the pension system ensure that younger teachers get lower pay than they otherwise would. This is probably where the idea that teachers are low paid comes from, but once again the culprit is union demands.

Joel Klein works us through the implications:

> Today in New York City, for example, the average annual per-teacher compensation is more than $110,000. The salary portion is $71,000, and the pension portion is $23,000. (The rest is for health insurance, FICA and other benefits.) A mix that was more typical of what exists in the private sector would help us attract more qualified people into teaching— and keep them there during the first five years, when we traditionally lose a third or more.

Here is an example of what that means. New York City's starting salary for teachers is $45,000, and the increases in the early years are low. If instead we started teachers at $52,000 or $55,000, gave them bigger increases in the early years, and paid for it by reducing their pensions, we would attract and keep better teachers.

As Chancellor, Joel Klein tried to reform the pay structure in New York "based on discussion with many new and prospective teachers." He wanted to offer new teachers a choice: they could have the current salary and benefit package or one that was front-weighted with a higher salary and lower pension benefits. Though the choice was entirely left to the new hires, "the teachers union rejected the offer, calling it 'anti-union.'"

The unions, of course, jealously guard the privilege of making pension decisions for their members, because it increases the union's power.

Another thing that unions have done is install such draconian seniority provisions in contracts that when school districts decide they have to cut teacher positions, it's often keen, high-performing young teachers who get cut first rather than burned-out senior teachers coasting to retirement. A particularly depressing example of this happened in Los Angeles recently.

The Westlake neighborhood of Los Angeles is an impoverished area. Until 2007, it had been served by some of the lowest-performing schools in the city. But then John H. Liechty Middle School opened with, according to the *Los Angeles Times*, "a seasoned principal, dozens of energetic young teachers and a mission to 'reinvent education' in the nation's second-largest school district."[8] Results came quickly, with the students' scores on standardized tests showing excellent improvement in English and math. Teachers were being rated according to their ability to boost test scores, and many were in the top quintile in the district.

At the end of 2009, however, budget cuts necessitated the release of half the school's teachers, seventeen of whom were in that top quintile. The result, according to the *Times*: "By the end of the last school year, Liechty had plummeted from first to 61st—near the bottom among middle schools—in raising English scores and fallen out of the top 10 in boosting math scores." The good teachers were released because of decades-old seniority clauses embedded in teachers' contracts.

The *Times* was somewhat upset by this, and, in an admirable display of investigative reporting, broadened the scope of its story. It investigated how the dismissal, over the previous two years, of about 1,000 teachers, all discharged on the basis of lack of seniority, had affected the district's schools. Its findings make sad reading:

> Because seniority is largely unrelated to performance, the district has laid off hundreds of its most promising math and English teachers. About 190 ranked in the top fifth in raising scores and more than 400 ranked in the top 40%.
>
> Schools in some of the city's poorest areas were disproportionately hurt by the layoffs. Nearly one in 10 teachers in South Los Angeles schools was laid off, nearly twice the rate

in other areas. Sixteen schools lost at least a fourth of their teachers, all but one of them in South or Central Los Angeles.

Far fewer teachers would be laid off if the district were to base the cuts on performance rather than seniority. The least experienced teachers also are the lowest-paid, so more must be laid off to meet budgetary targets. An estimated 25% more teachers would have kept their jobs if L.A. Unified had based its cuts on teachers' records in improving test scores.

What is particularly ironic about the Liechty dismissals is that most of the laid-off teachers were active union members. When they received their pink slips, they asked what the union was going to do to help them. The United Teachers Los Angeles President, A. J. Duffy, rebuffed them, saying he told them, "There was no evidence that new teachers do better than veterans; moreover, seniority-based layoffs were part of union policy." Teachers present at the meeting say he told them that making exceptions to the seniority clauses would be "an act of disloyalty."

The school district actually took the laid-off teachers' side, for the reason the *Times* mentioned above: laying off senior teachers would mean fewer lay-offs in all. The union refused to budge, but graciously allowed the laid-off teachers to claim seniority as substitute teachers, which in turn led to complaints from senior teachers already on the substitute list.

Of course, the layoffs left Liechty without enough teachers, so some had to be hired to fill the void. Who replaced the keen young teachers? Many of the candidates for this Middle School were elementary school teachers who had been laid off elsewhere, but who had enough seniority to require placement in another school. The result was teachers without the interest or experience, despite their seniority, in teaching middle school students from a poor background. The *Times* reported that some replacement teachers "left in tears within days or called in sick every day." One successful teacher who quit in frustration said, "The teachers who were hired didn't want the jobs, and those who wanted them weren't allowed to teach." Classrooms saw as many as ten substitute teachers over the year. Many of the subs had no credentials or experience in the subjects they were supposed to be teaching.

With the quality of teaching suffering, students simply stopped paying attention. Eventually, the *students* sued the school district, alleging that seniority-based cuts damaged their right to an equitable education. A judge granted a preliminary injunction stopping further lay-offs, and district officials are working on a settlement, but that is opposed by the union. Thanks to the union's intransigence, the students are still suffering:

> "We do the same lesson over and over again," said Jana Medina, an eighth-grader who has had three substitute teachers in history alone. "I feel like I'm not learning anything."
>
> Jana got a C in history last year in a different middle school, according to her report card. Last term she got an F. Her mother, Lourdes Gonzalez, said she went to talk to one of the substitutes, but the teacher barely knew who Jana was.
>
> "We live in a very hard area," Gonzalez said. "The only way to break out is through education, and she's not getting a good one now."

Indeed, but whoever said teachers' unions were interested in education?

Eliminate Music, Not Administrators

Remember the Bill with No Name? As I said, the final purpose of the bill was to establish a federal slush fund for states that were facing shortfalls in their education budgets. I say slush fund, because the bill did not direct the payments to be used for improving the quality of education but for any and all education-related purposes, including salary increases.

An astonishing example of how local education bureaucrats used the money stems from Loudoun County, Virginia, just to the west of

Washington, D.C., where they used it to pay teachers to work less. According to the *Washington Post*:

> This bizarre turn of events began in April [2010], when the cash-strapped Loudoun County School Board approved a two-day Thanksgiving-week furlough for teachers. The measure saved $4.5 million. For students, it was not a major sacrifice, since Loudoun's school year is already longer than the state requires. But teachers were incensed and threatened to picket. Then, as one school board member put it, "along came this money from the federal Department of Education." Seizing the opportunity to mollify its teachers without cutting the budget, the school board decided to spend $4.5 million of the federal aid to restore two days' teacher pay. But since it was too late to redo the school schedule, teachers—and students—will still spend two fewer days in the classroom.[9]

If little ole Loudoun County could pay teachers not to teach for two days, it should come as no surprise that New York City could do it for months, even years on end. Teachers there who are accused of misconduct—anything from lying to a hearing to sexual harassment—are sent to sit around on full pay:

> Because their union contract makes it extremely difficult to fire them, the teachers have been banished by the school system to its "rubber rooms"—off-campus office space where they wait months, even years, for their disciplinary hearings.
>
> The 700 or so teachers can practice yoga, work on their novels, paint portraits of their colleagues—pretty much anything but school work. They have summer vacation just like their classroom colleagues and enjoy weekends and holidays through the school year.

"You just basically sit there for eight hours," said Orlando Ramos, who spent seven months in a rubber room, officially known as a temporary reassignment center, in 2004-05. "I saw several near-fights. 'This is my seat.' 'I've been sitting here for six months.' That sort of thing."[10]

The city's Department of Education puts the cost of these "rubber rooms" to the taxpayer at $65 million a year. Los Angeles has a similar system, with 168 educators in it.

School districts love to threaten teacher lay-offs during a budget crisis. It's one of the oldest tricks in the public sector playbook—when asked to make cuts, always threaten to cut the thing the public finds most valuable. Not surprisingly, when Wellesley, Massachusetts, faced a school budget crisis in January 2011, Superintendent Bella T. Wong threatened to slash the budgets for school libraries, as well as art, music, physical education, and humanities classes.[11] Not on the chopping block: the school district's overpaid bureaucrats, sixty of whom are among the top 100 highest paid public employees in the town. In 2009, Superintendent Bella T. Wong made $169,000 in her first year in the job. Wellesley, according to the 2000 census, has fewer than 27,000 people. The school district has one high school, one middle school, one preschool, and seven elementary schools, which require no fewer than thirty-four district administrators (including, on the district website, the various directors' secretaries) led by Superintendent Wong.

It's the administrators, as ever, who make the big bucks in the education bureaucracy. Take Jackson County, Michigan, where thirty-nine school district employees take home more than $100,000—all but three of them bureaucrats. One Superintendent earned more than $177,000.[12] It is not just the natural tendency of bureaucrats to feather their own nests; the increasing federal role in education means that bureaucrats at every level of government are helping each other in this process, so that school district administrators are needed to manage federal dollars and are far too valuable to fire when there are libraries to close and music teachers to lay off. After all, it's all about the children, or so they say.

The No Child Left Behind (NCLB) Act of 2001 increased federal education spending by 41 percent between 2001 and 2008; it also, as Brad Lips and Evan Feinberg of the Heritage Foundation noted, "created new rules and regulations for schools and significantly increased compliance costs for state and local governments. According to the Office of Management and Budget, No Child Left Behind increased state and local governments' annual paperwork burden by 6,680,334 hours, at an estimated cost of $141 million dollars."[13]

Some states have their own estimates of the costs—and they are staggering. According to Communities for Quality Education, the Virginia Department of Education put the cost of administering NCLB at $248 million from 2005 through 2008, over and above the support received from the federal government. New Mexico's study found an extra expense of $94 million for 2003 to 2005, while Connecticut found extra costs of $42 million—just three school districts in the state cost an extra $23 million. All these costs were unmet by the federal government.

In Hawaii, a study for the legislature found that the total cost of NCLB would be $191 million from 2003 to 2008, with an additional $25 million to develop the program. In Minnesota, the State Auditor found that the testing of students with disabilities and limited knowledge of English alone would cost $19 million annually. In Ohio, the figure was astronomical. A 2003 study found that the state would need $1.4 billion annually to meet the costs of NCLB through the 2013–2014 school year.

This is actually just an escalation of a problem caused by federal interference in education that started in 1965 with the Elementary and Secondary Education Act of that year. In 1994, a General Accounting Office survey estimated that there were 13,400 federally funded full-time positions in the states working to implement federal education programs.[14] That was three times the number of employees then working at the federal Department of Education. Between 1965 and 2005, taxpayers invested about $778 billion in these programs.

Lips and Feinberg quantified exactly what that meant for state education departments:

> The same [GAO] report found that state education agencies were forced to reserve a far greater share of federal than state funds for state-level use—by a ratio of 4 to 1—due to the administrative and regulatory burden of federal programs. Because it cost so much more to allocate a federal dollar than a state dollar, 41 percent of the financial support and staffing of state education agencies was a product of federal dollars and regulations. In other words, the federal government was the cause of 41 percent of the administrative burden at the state level despite providing just 7 percent of overall education funding.[15]

Small wonder there are so many administrators essentially immune to firing.

Grade Inflation, Standards Deflation

The education establishment often points to rising grades to justify this high spending, but when you look closely at the issue, you find that we've actually suffered a two decade-plus period of grade inflation, not rising standards.

In 2005, ACT, the nonprofit organization that administers what used to be known as the Advanced College Testing Program, but is now generally known as the ACT Test, published a study that sought to establish whether or not grade inflation had taken place over the period 1991–2003. They did this by comparing high school GPAs to the results of the standardized ACT test. They found that during that time, GPAs had increased by between 6 percent and 12.5 percent over the ACT test results.[16]

A *Pittsburgh Post-Gazette* survey in 2007 found that, "Grades—some weighted with extra points or fractions of points for taking harder courses—are getting so high that a solid B is becoming the new C, which years ago was considered average." The paper backed this up with some worrying examples:

- Seniors at Pine-Richland High School who have a weighted grade point average below 3.3—a B—are in the bottom half of the class.
- At Mt. Lebanon High School, roughly 20 percent of the senior class of about 470 students have weighted grade point averages of 4.6 or higher, and averages occasionally reach as high as 5.2.
- Over a decade at Allegheny College, the number of applicants with grade point averages greater than 4.0 grew from 1 in 10 in 1996 to nearly 1 in 5 in 2006. In that time, the average grade point average of applicants rose from 4.04 to 4.18.[17]

The Post-Gazette found plenty of evidence of grade inflation out there. A 2007 study by UCLA's Higher Education Research Institute traced the inflation back to at least 1987, and commented that "nearly half of freshmen reported high school grade point averages of A–or higher in 2006, compared with 19.4 percent in 1966." Another study of freshmen who sat the SAT in 2006 found that grades had gone up as SAT scores remained the same or even dropped.

Grade inflation is great for bureaucrats because it justifies their programs (and the inevitable expansion of those programs) while also getting outraged parents off their back, because who can complain about good report cards. The real losers are the students who have no real measure of how they are performing academically, or worse, are being given an inflated sense of their achievement.

Grade inflation, however, is a problem for college admissions—how do you choose between literally thousands of students with 4.0 GPAs? In 2006, UCLA received 47,317 applications, of which nearly 21,000 had GPAs of 4.0—or above.

Jess Lord, dean of admissions and financial aid at Haverford College in Pennsylvania told the Associated Press, "We're seeing 30, 40 valedictorians at a high school because they don't want to create these distinctions between students."[18] That in turn causes problems for the students. As the AP found:

> In Georgia, high school grades rose after the state began awarding HOPE scholarships to students with a 3.0 high school GPA. But the scholarship requires students to keep a 3.0 GPA in college, too, and more than half who received the HOPE in the fall of 1998 and entered the University of Georgia system lost eligibility before earning 30 credits. Next year, Georgia is taking a range of steps to tighten eligibility, including calculating GPA itself rather than relying on schools, and no longer giving extra GPA weight to vaguely labeled "honors" classes.[19]

The irony is that if grade inflation is a problem in high schools, it seems to be worse in colleges. Duke University's Stuart Rojstaczer has been following the problem since 2003, when he wrote an op-ed on the subject for the *Washington Post*:

> How rare is the C in college? The data indicate that not only is C an endangered species but that B, once the most popular grades at universities and colleges, has been supplanted by the former symbol of perfection, the A.
>
> For example, at Duke, which all evidence indicates is not a "leader" in grade inflation—by a long shot—C's now make up less than 10 percent of all grades. In 1969 the C was a

respectable thing, given more than one-quarter of the time.
A's overcame B's to reach the top of the charts in grade popu-
larity in the early 1990s.

At Pomona College, C's are now less than 4 percent of all
grades. About half of all grades at Pomona, Duke, Harvard
and Columbia are in the A range. State schools are not
immune to this change. At the University of Illinois, A's con-
stitute more than 40 percent of all grades and outnumber C's
by almost three to one. (More information on this subject can
be found at www.gradeinflation.com.)

This trend of the dominance of the A and the diminution
of the C began in the 1960s, abated somewhat in the '70s and
came back strong in the '80s. The previous signs of academic
disaster, D and F, went by the wayside in the Vietnam era,
when flunking out meant becoming eligible for the draft. At
Duke, Pomona, Harvard and elsewhere, D's and F's combined
now represent about 2 percent of all grades given.[20]

The evidence is overwhelming that grade inflation has significantly
devalued the academic worth of college education. Professors have an
incentive not to give realistic grades, because if they do, their enrollment
will drop and, thanks to the higher education funding system, they will
suffer as a result. A 2009 article for the National Association of Scholars
(NAS) reveals the effect of such easy marking:

A recent survey of more than 30,000 first year students
revealed that nearly half were spending more hours drinking
than they were studying. Researchers from the University of
California, Irvine found that a third of students surveyed
expected B's just for attending class, and 40 percent said they
deserved a B for completing the assigned reading....

Not long ago, at UWM [University of Wisconsin-Milwau-
kee], an astronomy professor observed that up to half of one

class "failed to show up most of the time." A physics professor on that campus noted the many students who stopped
attending and never took the final examination. "One would
think this is a motivational issue," he said. John Merrow, an
expert on these matters, writes, "Students everywhere report
that they average only 10-15 hours of academic work outside
of class per week and are able to attain 'B' or better grade-
point averages."[21]

Finally, another cause of grade inflation might be ideological indoctrination: repeat back the "politically correct" answers and get an A. With
college faculty overwhelmingly on the left of the political—and cultural—
spectrum, college professors often view their lecture theaters as the front
line in winning the culture war, converting students to pacifism, socialism,
feminism, moral relativism, and any number of race-based "isms"
(remember Eric Mar?). No less a figure than Harvard's Harvey Mansfield
believes that faculty members routinely give inflated grades to those who
parrot their ideological beliefs back at them. The Foundation for Individual Rights in Education (FIRE) records the lack of ideological diversity
on college campuses. A visit to its website makes for disheartening reading for an open-minded parent.

This is a phenomenon in desperate need of study, but campus administrators, who are generally on the Left themselves, would be the last
people to conduct such a survey. As the NAS says, "Imagine a chancellor
or president giving a graduation address that condemns professors on
campus for their overly generous grading. It simply will not happen."
The opposite is likely to be true: lower standards and higher grades attract
more state funding.

In case you're wondering who pays the bill for political indoctrination
and slack teaching and grading standards at state schools—well, you
guessed right: it's you. The bill has grown so huge that some economists
and higher education watchers are likening higher education budgets and
tuition charges to a stock market bubble.

Higher Ed Gets Ready to Pop

If teachers are well paid when taking all their benefits into account, what about university lecturers and tenured professors? Such "post-secondary teachers," according to the Bureau of Labor Statistics, earn $49.88 an hour. They total 1,601 hours of work for an average annual salary of just under $80,000. If they worked the 2,000 hours that managers typically do, they would earn just under $100,000, compared to the manager's average of $83,000. That makes them more highly paid than any public sector management profession except engineering managers ($107,000) and Chief Executives ($120,000), but remember that that is the average for all postsecondary teachers, including those just setting out on the tenure track. The hourly wage has also increased 20 percent since 2004.

Thanks to the massive amounts of federal money shoved towards earth sciences departments—driven in large part by global warming programs, a good example of how federal dollars help skew research— "atmospheric, earth, marine and space science teachers" are the highest paid of any lecturers except law school professors, at $70.61 for 1,471 hours of work. That translates to a manager-equivalent salary of $141,000, outranking even the median private sector CEO. Back in 2004, by the way, they earned just $53 an hour, so their salary has gone up 32 percent. Every time they show *An Inconvenient Truth* to their students, they must offer up a silent "thank you" to Al Gore.

Interestingly, there is not much regional variation in these figures. Lecturers in the Boston area—which encompasses Harvard and MIT, to name but two of the exclusive universities in the vicinity—earn just slightly more at $50.97 an hour.

With salaries like these—not to mention the healthcare benefits, retirement plans, and job security—it is no wonder that massive amounts of money are needed to run the nation's higher education system. On top of state and federal grants, the way that the education system has been funded over the past few decades has been via federally guaranteed student loans, with privately-funded loans also playing a part. In the

2008–2009 academic year, students and their families borrowed $95 billion to pay for higher education.

Borrowing has reached such a vast amount because, as a recent survey in *Money* magazine found, "After adjusting for financial aid, the amount families pay for college has skyrocketed 439 percent since 1982....Normal supply and demand can't begin to explain cost increases of this magnitude."

The financial web site Seeking Alpha looked at the trends and identified three phases in cost inflation: 1990 to 1993, 2000 to 2004, and 2007 onwards. These three periods all roughly coincide with periods of domestic recession. During healthier economic times, tuition fees increased at about the same rate as household income, "suggesting that US higher learning institutions have been the beneficiaries of a remarkable amount of insulation from economic circumstances during these periods."[22]

That insulation has in part been provided by the federal government subsidizing student loans. Until the passage of the Obamacare act, virtually every student loan was guaranteed by the government and so could be offered at a couple of percentage points lower interest rate than the private sector would provide. Obamacare has ended that, viewing it rightly as a subsidy to the banks administering the loans; but rather than getting the government out of the loan business altogether, it has instead expanded the Feds' role as a direct provider of student loans.

However, as Glenn Reynolds, a law professor at the University of Tennessee, has pointed out, the rapid increase in tuition fees has created a bubble very similar to the real estate bubble of the 2000s:

> The buyers think what they're buying will appreciate in value, making them rich in the future. The product grows more and more elaborate, and more and more expensive, but the expense is offset by cheap credit provided by sellers eager to encourage buyers to buy.
>
> Buyers see that everyone else is taking on mounds of debt, and so are more comfortable when they do so themselves;

besides, for a generation, the value of what they're buying has gone up steadily. What could go wrong? Everything continues smoothly until, at some point, it doesn't....

Bubbles burst when there are no longer enough excessively optimistic and ignorant folks to fuel them. And there are signs that this is beginning to happen already.[23]

Those signs include more and more graduates realizing that their degrees in "religious and women's studies" are not the ticket to a high-paying job they were promised. Moreover, monthly payments of $700 on the student loan can be extremely problematic when searching for the sort of job that isn't there.

Another sign is the spreading awareness that some universities are "dropout factories," where dropout rates even from well-qualified high school graduates can approach 90 percent or more. Other colleges are well known as party schools, where meeting the national average of more time drinking than studying would have you labeled as a hard-working nerd. When parents and students sober up to this fact, will they still be willing to take on loans to pay for four years of parties—when there might not be a high-paying job at the end to pay the tab?

Finally, it appears increasingly that the best jobs on Wall Street and the like are going only to those who graduate from the elite schools. In effect, high-profile, high-paying firms have outsourced their recruitment practices to the admissions departments of the Ivy League schools. Lauren Rivera, a management professor at Kellogg School of Management at Northwestern University, detailed exactly this practice in a recent paper:

I find that educational credentials were the most common criteria employers used to solicit and screen resumes. However, it was not the content of education that elite employers valued but rather its prestige. Employers privileged candidates who possessed a super-elite (e.g., top 5) university affiliation and attributed superior cognitive, cultural, and moral qualities to candidates who had been admitted to such an institution, regardless of their actual performance once there.

A candidate had to pass that test before recruiters examined the next most important criterion—extracurricular activities. To make the grade, going to a famous, but not super-elite, school wasn't enough:

> So-called "public Ivies" such as University of Michigan and Berkeley were not considered elite or even prestigious in the minds of evaluators (in contrast, these "state schools" were frequently described pejoratively as "safety schools" that were "just okay"). Even Ivy League designation was insufficient for inclusion in the super-elite. For undergraduate institutions, "top-tier" typically included only Harvard, Princeton, Yale, Stanford, and potentially Wharton (University of Pennsylvania's Business School). By contrast, Brown, Cornell, Dartmouth, and University of Pennsylvania (general studies) were frequently described as "second tier" schools that were filled primarily with candidates who "didn't get in" to a super-elite school.
>
> Definitions of "top-tier" were even narrower for professional schools, primarily referring to Yale, Harvard, Stanford, and to a lesser extent Columbia law schools, and Harvard, Wharton (University of Pennsylvania), and Stanford business schools. A consulting director (white, female) illustrates, "Going to a major university is important. Being at the big top four schools is important. Even it's a little more important being at Harvard or Stanford [for MBAs]; you know it's just better chances for somebody." A consultant (Asian-American, male) described of being at a "top" school, "It's light-years different whether or not we are going to consider your resume."

Yet even these recruiters, who regard the university as of prime importance, discount the teaching received at the university:

> Evaluators relied so intensely on "school" as a criterion of evaluation not because they believed that the content of elite curricula better prepared students for life in their firms—in fact, evaluators tended to believe that elite and, in particular, super-elite instruction was "too abstract," "overly theoretical," or even "useless" compared to the more "practical" and "relevant" training offered at "lesser" institutions—but rather due to the strong cultural meanings and character judgments evaluators attributed to admission and enrollment at an elite school.

In other words, the universities added no value bar the simple fact of selecting someone to attend the university. From the rest of Rivera's research, it is clear that what these recruiters are after is brain-power, not an education, and accepted that top-tier schools did that sorting for them.

Moreover, the recruiters were more impressed with super-elite graduates who had done things besides get an education:

> Those without significant extracurricular experiences or those who participated in activities that were primarily academically or pre-professionally oriented were perceived to be "boring," "tools," "bookworms," or "nerds" who might turn out to be "corporate drones" if hired. A consultant (white, male) articulated the essence of this sentiment: "We like to interview at schools like Harvard and Yale, but people who have like 4.0s and are in the engineering department but you know don't have any friends, have huge glasses, read their textbooks all day, those people have no chance here....I have always said, [my firm] is like a fraternity of smart people."

What all this suggests is that the old idea of getting a good education to get a good job is out-of-date. Getting a good job now in America is strikingly reminiscent of the old City establishment in imperial London, when you got the job if you had gone to Oxford or Cambridge and were seen as being "clubbable" or "a good chap."

So what exactly is the point of higher education these days? It appears to have degenerated into a meaningless ritual, one of high grades (especially if you toe the line of the leftist pontificating professors), little work, and little in the way of traditional reward, all paid for by the taxpayer either by direct college funding or via subsidized loans, which allows college lecturers to receive an extremely good compensation package. And because the good private sector job might not be there when a student graduates, more and more of them are hoping to join the cosseted professors in the academy—the tenured position with the great salary and few hours. There has been a vast expansion of Ph.D. programs that cater to the federal-loan subsidized perpetual student. The result is what Harvard professor Louis Menand calls "the Ph.D. Problem" of far too many doctoral students chasing too few tenured positions; and they take their time doing it. In the 1960s, graduate students generally took between four to six years to acquire a Ph.D. Today, it ranges from about seven to eleven years, or almost double the time. I have to say I find this astonishing. When I was considering studying for a D.Phil. at Oxford University, the general expectation was that the thesis would be finished and the degree awarded within three or four years (the UK public funding body *reduces* funding to institutions that take longer). All this time in graduate school (often without gaining a Ph.D., or if gaining a Ph.D., without a tenure-track job) represents a gross misallocation of intelligence. Yet, according to Menand, the students actually like this:

> Students continue to check into the doctoral motel, and they
> don't seem terribly eager to check out. They like being in a
> university, and, since there is usually plenty of demand for

their quite inexpensive teaching, universities like having them. Business is good. Where is the problem? ...

What is clear is that students who spend eight or nine years in graduate school are being seriously over-trained for the jobs that are available. The argument that they need the training to be qualified to teach undergraduates is belied by the fact that they are already teaching undergraduates. Undergraduate teaching is part of doctoral education; at many institutions, graduate students begin teaching classes the year they arrive. And the idea that the doctoral thesis is a rigorous requirement is belied by the quality of most doctoral theses. If every graduate student were required to publish a single peer-reviewed article instead of writing a thesis, the net result would probably be a plus for scholarship.

But of course, this begs the question of whether they are really being "over-trained" or whether they are actually enjoying a highly attractive form of welfare for bright people, given that they are supported by taxpayer-financed loans and positions. Higher education has become, in essence, a playground for a self-selected elite. They spend massive amounts of money—much of it obtained from the taxpayer via the grant process—in training themselves, and at the end of the process they receive one of the best-compensated jobs around, and again stick you with the bill.

In that respect, tenured professors at state schools aren't alone. It seems that government employment has become the goal for many college graduates. In 2010, a consulting firm named Universum asked 59,500 college students from 345 universities who their ideal employer was. Google made the top of the list, but the State Department, FBI, CIA, and NASA all came in the top ten. For engineers, the Department of Energy was the seventh most popular dream employer. As Washington, D.C., news station WTOP reported proudly, "Federal agencies had their strongest showing among humanities and liberal arts majors, with [government-supported] Teach for America leading the list, followed by the State Department, Walt Disney, Google and the Peace Corps. The top ten also included the FBI, CIA and NIH, with the National Security Agency in 11th place."

Parents agree, too. A recent poll found that nearly half of *Republicans* would recommend a federal or government job to a new college graduate. Over 70 percent of Democrats would do the same. The *Washington Post* found one man who summed up the sentiment: "Why not?" asked Nirmal Sandhu, 56, the father of two college students, who emigrated from India to Long Island in 1987. "Working in the federal government is a good job. For my kids, I think it would be great."[24]

In fact, the Census Bureau's Current Population Survey suggests that government employed more college graduates in 2009–2010 than any other sector. The public sector increased its share of college graduates by 107,000 in that period, while manufacturing and finance cut their number of graduate hires by 46,000 and 71,000 respectively.[25]

Government jobs have obvious attractions: they offer good pay, an extremely low risk of getting fired, excellent benefits, and the self-flattery that one is engaged in "public service." Rather than actually educating people, the education establishment seems to have defined its primary end as producing more trainee bureaucrats. So we have a system that lures our brightest children out of the productive sector and into the public sector, where they can live off the taxes of all the hard-working suckers who actually produce and manufacture and contribute to our economy. Welcome to the road to serfdom.

A PROGRAM FOR PUBLIC SECTOR REFORM

So what can we do? The great thing about America is that it is founded on ideas rather than on blood or soil. This means that when things go wrong, we can look back to our founding for possible solutions. Just as the Founders revolted against a long list of injuries and usurpations, so should we. Our form of government—the regulatory state of the robber barons—has become destructive of the ends of life, liberty, and the pursuit of happiness, and so we should return to the central principle of limited government as best securing the freedoms our nation was founded to honor. A simple but effective program of reducing the size and scope of government is necessary, one that can be accomplished in but a few years.

It is essential that this program be regarded as a package of ideas, each one complementing the others. Applying the program in a piecemeal fashion will allow those opposed to government reform to block each reform as it comes up. As Margaret Thatcher found when she tackled the problem in the UK, government reform must be sweeping and comprehensive: sweeping so that the supporters of bureaucracy have no time to dig in; and comprehensive so that they cannot retreat to redoubts and entrench there. For instance, in my opinion, Mrs. Thatcher's two greatest mistakes in her otherwise comprehensive reform of the British public sector were, first, to ignore the European Union, which has since become the main driver of British regulation, and second, failing to privatize the BBC, which, with its dominant state-supported status on the radio and television airwaves, has become a tool for the bureaucracy to perpetuate itself, promulgating leftist views and indoctrinating the British public with the idea that Thatcherism is evil.

This program of reform I propose is not a detailed one—because this book isn't the proper place for policy-wonkery—but in its general terms, it should provide an example of the size and scope of what we need to do.

Shrink the Federal Government

Attempting to reduce the size of government program-by-program is almost certainly a fool's errand. With a trillion dollar deficit looming every year, ending earmarks or finding even $60 billion of "wasteful" programs is not going to help much. There needs to be an immediate and radical reduction in the size of government and its functions.

Whole government Departments need to be swept away. Foremost among these should be the Department of Commerce, which is where Big Government started. Those agencies it supervises that have a genuine and/or constitutional role (like the Census Bureau) can be spun off as executive agencies. Its international trade functions should be transferred to the Treasury Department.

Also on the chopping block should be the Departments of Energy, Labor, and Education. Energy should be provided and regulated by the free market—perhaps the Department's last function should be to abolish energy monopolies around the country. The best way to find energy solutions that will actually work in a cost-effective, practical way is to let private businesses compete to find them. Energy subsidies only retard our ability to become energy independent, because they divert taxpayer capital to inefficient, uneconomic, and politically favored projects, or simply bribe oil, gas, and coal companies to put up with burdensome regulations. We don't need more wind farms that slaughter more birds and blot more landscapes than they produce actual energy, and we don't need more biofuels that jack up the cost of food and waste more energy than they produce. All such energy subsidies should be abolished.

As for the Labor Department, its mission statement, which can be found on its webpage, is "to foster, promote, and develop the welfare of the wage earners, job seekers, and retirees of the United States; improve working conditions; advance opportunities for profitable employment; and assure work-related benefits and rights." In other words, the department has no valid constitutional function. It is a meddlesome bureaucracy trying to butt in on an economy that can work perfectly fine without it, and it spends $120 billion a year, which if refunded to the taxpayer along with the abolition of the department would do more for labor and stimulating the creation of jobs than anything the Obama administration has yet done.

Meanwhile the Department of Education could better be titled the Department of Misallocating Education Dollars, as its real function appears to be that of a vacuum that sucks up taxpayer dollars to distribute to fellow education bureaucrats around the country—who then put their own interests ahead of our children's interests. A decade ago, abolishing the department was part of the Republican party's platform. It should be front and center in the public square once again. Writing in the *Washington Examiner*, columnist Mona Charen reminds us that abolishing the Department of Education isn't extreme, it is what any rational government reformer would do. The Department of Education exists primarily, like other bureaucracies, continually to expand its reach:

Busy bureaucrats have created reams of paperwork for teachers and administrators, pushed dubious curricula like bilingual education, and adopted manifold extra-educational missions. The department's website lists hundreds of programs that bear little to no relation to schooling, including the "Spinal Cord Injuries Model Systems Program," "Small Business Innovation Research Program," "Protection and Advocacy of Individual Rights," "Predominantly Black Institutions Program," "Life Skills for State and Local Prisoners," "Institute for International Public Policy," "Grants to States to Improve Management of Drug and Violence Prevention Programs," "Grants to Reduce Alcohol Abuse," and "Developing Hispanic-Serving Institutions Program," to name just a handful. No one checks. There is no accountability. There are no consequences for failure, except perhaps, requests for even greater funding next year.[1]

Parents are the primary educators of their children—that is their responsibility, and it is a responsibility they can be empowered to execute more fully the more the funding and management of the schools is entirely a local proposition. Hey, federal bureaucrats—leave our kids alone!

Also on the chopping block should be the Department of Housing and Urban Development and the Department of Health and Human Services. Housing and urban development is the business of building contractors and local communities; it is not a rightful, or necessary, function of the federal government; and whatever is usefully done by the Department of Health and Human Services would certainly be better and more efficiently done at the state or even the local level—closer to the people it is meant to serve.

Recharter Executive Agencies

There are some agencies that are mightier than government departments, such as the Environmental Protection Agency and the Food and Drug Administration. These should be reined in by reducing their regulatory powers and by new congressional charters strictly enumerating what they can do—and the level of service to be provided to the taxpayer. Enforcement should be left to district attorneys, courts, and due process. No agency should ever treat an American citizen as a potential criminal rather than as a customer worthy of respect. The bureaucracy works best that is entitled to do the least.

Reform Federal Pay and Conditions

We need to overhaul how federal workers are paid: automatic pay raises need to go, as do seniority-based pay scales, and the virtual immunity of federal workers from being fired. Working for the federal government should not be a way to get gold-plated benefits and a salary you couldn't match in the private sector. We need to get back to the idea of "public service," where government workers—on the public payroll—don't make more than taxpayers in comparable jobs. Unaffordable government pension schemes should be phased out and replaced by a 403(b) plan—the non-profit version of the 401(k).

Tackle Entitlement Spending

As Nick Gillespie and Veronique de Rugy pointed out in *Reason* magazine, America's entitlement programs (most notably Social Security, Medicare, and Medicaid) are the product of a very different America, where it was assumed that the elderly were at particular risk of falling into poverty.[2] Seniors today are among the wealthiest people in America; and though entitlements once given are hard to take away, the simple fact is that elderly Americans have no need for universal entitlements. Moreover, our government can't afford it. Life expectancy has increased sharply, meaning that more seniors are claiming more benefits for longer than the system can possibly sustain.

Gillespie and de Rugy have a simple and sensible suggestion for tackling Social Security:

Congress should cut benefits today for people who are 55 and younger. Those individuals still have plenty of time to adjust their expectations about future benefits and plan for retirement. We should gradually raise the initial age of eligibility to at least 70 and progressively increase it to track life expectancy (currently almost 79). We should also means-test these programs so that only those who really need the help get it. Such changes are relatively easy to implement and would allow lawmakers to pass reforms that won't kick in until years down the road.

Medicaid (which is means-tested) should be given over to the states and local government to administer, with the funds transferred by the U.S. Treasury in the form of block grants. As Gillespie and de Rugy point out, "Because they are closer to the actual beneficiaries, more knowledgeable about regional differences in the target population, and more responsive to local needs, state and local governments are better suited to take care of poor people." Moreover, as was proven in welfare reform, state and local governments can innovate and experiment with better ways of delivering services to the poor.

The final giant entitlement program is Medicare. Republican Congressman Paul Ryan of Wisconsin has suggested some radical and practical reforms to Medicare that will significantly reduce its burden on the taxpayer and increase individual responsibility. Instead of the government paying doctors and hospitals directly, the government would fund the Medicare recipient to the tune of around $11,000 annually. The recipient could then purchase a private health plan and use leftover funds in a Medical Savings Account (MSA). The MSA could be used for non-covered medical payments or to purchase long-term care.[3] This proposal would assuredly increase competition among health plan providers by opening up a huge new market. Moreover, it would slash the cost of administering Medicare.

Make Contracts Public and Abolish Grants

The Office of Personnel Management should be required to find out how many people government contractors employ on a government contact; and the Office for Management and Budget should have the power to revoke contracts that are poor value for money: this would expose the "shadow government" of government contractors to light.

Research grants should be abolished because they reward ideas for research rather than the results of research, and are easily abused for patronage. Instead, the government should award substantial prizes for outstanding practical research that has delivered results. With government out of the research grant business, more research dollars will come from private investors looking for a return on their investment and philanthropic bodies for whom the prize will be important as much for its prestige as for its dollar awards. Science will be less skewed by political considerations and much more dedicated to finding scientific solutions to public problems.

Introduce a Single Fair Tax

The first step to tax reform is recognizing that income should be taxed only once. At present we are taxed on our money when we earn it, when we try to save or invest it, when we purchase something (in most states) and when we try to leave it to our heirs on our death. When you think about it, that's pretty outrageous. Death taxes, capital gains taxes, and other additional taxes on our earnings should be abolished. What should take their place is a single, flat income tax where all income is taxed once, with everyone paying the same rate, with the revenues then being split between federal, state, and local government. Seven states—Colorado, Illinois, Massachusetts, Michigan, Pennsylvania, and Utah—and many Eastern European countries already operate under a flat tax; so we know it can work.

A flat tax could even serve as a social welfare program that avoids the problem of means-testing (where people can be discouraged from earning more income because it will cost them benefits). That was the suggestion of the great Nobel Prize-winning economist Milton Friedman, at least. Robert Frank summarized the suggestion in the *New York Times* shortly after Friedman's death:

> His proposal, which he called the negative income tax, was to replace the multiplicity of existing welfare programs with a single cash transfer—say, $6,000—to every citizen. A family of four with no market income would thus receive an annual payment from the I.R.S. of $24,000. For each dollar the family then earned, this payment would be reduced by some fraction—perhaps 50 percent. A family of four earning $12,000 a year, for example, would receive a net supplement of $18,000 (the initial $24,000 less the $6,000 tax on its earnings).[4]

Another form of flat tax, championed by publisher Steve Forbes, would tax consumption—defined as income minus savings—rather than income. Any of these suggestions—a pure flat tax, a flat tax with standard deductions, a negative income tax, or a flat consumption tax—could provide the basis for a rational tax system that would significantly reduce the powers, privileges, and size of the IRS.

We'd also need to secure the flat tax with a constitutional amendment or a rewrite of Congressional rules so that it would take a supermajority (66 percent of votes cast) to alter the terms of the flat tax or to introduce a new emergency tax. This would help us protect the flat tax from becoming the plaything of special interests looking to write in a whole new army of deductions, loopholes, exemptions, and exceptions.

In the meantime, Congress should consider passing another Taxpayer Bill of Rights. In 2007, the House Republican Study Committee proposed one that bears serious consideration. Its core principles are:

1. Taxpayers have a right to have a federal government that does not grow beyond their ability to pay for it.
2. Taxpayers have a right to receive back each dollar that they entrust to the government for their retirement.
3. Taxpayers have a right to expect the government to balance the budget without having their taxes raised.
4. Taxpayers have a right to a simple, fair tax code that they can understand.

Such a document, properly drafted, would do wonders for framing the subsequent debate about the flat tax. It should also empower the National Taxpayer Advocate to make simple changes to the way the IRS works to address taxpayer frustrations, which can then be approved by Congress.

We should also strongly consider abolishing the corporate income tax. Not only does America have one of the highest corporate income tax rates in the developed world, some have suggested it costs more to collect the tax than it raises in revenue. Abolition of the tax would be a massive stimulus for businesses and would make America much more attractive to investors. Companies would be able to reinvest the savings in expansion, higher wages, better conditions for employees, higher payouts for stockholders to attract more investment, or, most likely, a combination of all of this. The country's finances would not suffer much, if at all. The only loser would be the IRS.

Regulatory Reform

Congress needs to reassert control over the bureaucratic regulators. The first step should be to pass the REINS Act (the cute acronym stands for Regulations in Need of Scrutiny), which would require a congressional go-ahead for any major regulation that would impose significant costs on the economy. As said, however, that is a first step. Other measures are needed. My colleagues Wayne Crews and Ryan Young have outlined six such measures:[5]

- Appoint an annual bipartisan commission to comb through the books and suggest rules that deserve repeal. Congress would then vote up-or-down on the repeal package without amendment, to avoid behind-the-scenes deal-making.
- Require all new regulations to have built-in five-year sunset provisions. If Congress decides a rule is worth keeping, it can vote to extend it for another five years.
- Consider Senator Mark Warner's "one in, one out" proposal, which holds that for every new rule that hits the books, an old one must be repealed. (This reform is in the process of being introduced in the United Kingdom.)
- Let states take the lead, allowing 50 laboratories of democracy to continually discover more effective approaches through trial and error, subject to interstate competition.
- Hold agencies to higher standards when it comes to quantifying regulatory costs. To the extent that agencies do calculate costs, they tend to lowball them while highballing benefits. (This is particularly the case for the EPA, which, as already discussed, regularly finds trillions of dollars in benefits for their regulation, much to the amusement of professional economists.)
- Keep small businesses better informed about new rules. Few have the money to pay staff in Washington to keep an eye on the Federal Register, so new rules often come as a surprise. Regulations hit small businesses especially hard. Businesses with fewer than 20 employees pay $10,585 per employee per year in compliance costs. Firms with over 500 employees pay $7,755 per employee per year.

I would only add that agencies must in no cases be allowed to be both judge and jury when it comes to any of their powers. We have seen how the EPA is tasked both to compile the science on global warming and then to assess whether the results are accurate and whether they demand action—which is asking a regulatory agency if something needs more regulation. We shouldn't be surprised at the answer. The bureaucrats don't merit this power; the people's representatives, Congress, should decide.

End Labor Union Privileges

It is frankly ridiculous that people can be forced to pay dues to a union of which they aren't members, but from Wisconsin teachers to public employees across the country, this is often the case.

The first thing to do is to remove public sector union collective bargaining privileges. Franklin D. Roosevelt didn't think government workers should be allowed to organize into unions. Congress should recognize what Roosevelt recognized.

But in the event that Congress is too cowardly to act—imagine that—state and local governments should take the lead in revoking collective bargaining agreements. This will be met with ferocious opposition, as happened in Wisconsin, but it is a necessary step in reforming public sector pay and benefit arrangements. Wisconsin actually provides an important example of the cynicism of unions, in that they offered to sacrifice their members' pay and benefits in order to retain collective bargaining and the union dues that come with it. With collective bargaining in place, a union simply has to wait until a more favorable administration comes to power, presumably with the financial support of unions. It should be noted that there are no collective bargaining agreements for federal employees. This should become the norm across all levels of government.

Congress should repeal actions by the National Labor Relations Board (NLRB) that make it easier for unions to organize without the approval of a majority of the workers. Indeed, the powers of the NLRB should be significantly reduced to prevent such outrages as the NLRB General Counsel threatening to sue states that guaranteed citizens the right to a secret ballot in union elections. Similar reforms should be made to the National Mediation Board, which has a similar role for transportation industries.

Another reduction of union privilege would be paycheck protection measures. These provisions would allow workers to withhold any union dues that would be used for political purposes. James Sherk of the Heritage Foundation calculated that such protections would reduce union political contributions by about 50 percent.[6] That would be enough to significantly reduce the unhealthy influence of public sector unions on the election of their bosses.

With these privileges removed, public sector unions would have to reinvent themselves to provide real benefit to their members. One example would be to provide training opportunities to aid in their members' career development.[7]

This series of reforms would substantially alter the balance of power in state and local governments and allow agencies, police forces, education departments, fire departments, and so on to be shaped into genuine public service organizations rather than bilk-the-taxpayer operations.

Privatize Appropriate Government Functions

Many state and local public sector services might be better handled by the private or voluntary sector. Many local fire departments, for instance, are already run by private companies. Prisons, too, are often run on a private basis and have generally improved conditions for prisoners. Private schools have a long history of outperforming pubic schools—often at a far lower cost.

Reason magazine highlighted Sandy Springs, Georgia, whose city leaders "started with a blank slate" and asked "fundamental questions about what role government should play....Ultimately the city decided to 'buy' most services from the private sector." This decision has saved the residents of Sandy Springs "millions of dollars a year."[8]

Robert Nelson of the University of Maryland has also chronicled how neighborhood associations have been privatizing what had been the provinces of municipal government, de facto creating their own zoning laws and taking over services like snow removal, garbage collection, and so on, and providing such amenities as community swimming pools, golf courses, and landscaping. [9]

Nelson believes that there are two obstacles to the future expansion of "privatized neighborhoods" in established municipalities: the threat of "double taxation" from local government and a neighborhood association fee, and the lack of simple arrangements for such associations to form where local government is entrenched. States should pass laws encouraging neighborhood associations to take over as many responsibilities as possible from local government. The result, inevitably, will be lower costs, lower taxes, and more civic involvement.

Re-engineer Education

Ending collective bargaining arrangements and abolishing federal education programs will go a long way to reforming education. Equally fundamental is giving parents more choices on where they send their children to school. The local state school should not hold monopoly power over parents; state schools should have to compete for students. Wherever "school choice" has been tried—most notably in Sweden—it has been a significant success, reducing costs and bureaucracy while providing better quality education.

The Swedish system is based on giving parents a "voucher" that is equivalent in value to the average cost of educating a pupil at a local state school. Parents then use this voucher to purchase a place at a school of their choice. The funding follows the student, which means that public education supports the schools that are most popular with parents, which are, of course, the better schools. Schools that fail their students in whatever way lose students and therefore funding. Public school districts—and possibly individual schools—should also be free to set their own pay scales for teachers, preferably on a performance basis.

As for higher education, the financial aid system needs to be radically overhauled, and funding of public universities needs to be revised to reflect performance. That means, if universities receive public funds they need to be responsible to the taxpayer—college should not be a four-, five-, six-, or seven-year party, leaving students with a mountain of debt at the end. Graduates need to be prepared with skills for careers in the private, productive sector of the economy; they should not simply transition from the state-sponsored party of college to taxpayer-sponsored employment in government. State governments might also want to consider shifting their resources away from universities to vocational schools where the cost-benefit ratio might be more direct.

Finally, ending union collective bargaining agreements and replacing tenure with long-term contracts, as happened in the UK, should help rebalance lecturers' compensation arrangements and still secure academic freedom. As with teachers and civil servants, performance-related pay would be an important and motivating innovation.

Class War 2.0

There is an old joke about socialists that goes, "How many socialists does it need to change a lightbulb? None—it's the system that has to change."

It's clear that our current system needs to change. We cannot afford to let government robber barons continually expand their bureaucratic fiefdoms, battening on a long-suffering and shrinking class of taxpayers.

Taxpayers of the world, unite! What we need is a new class war—Class War 2.0—against the system that allows and encourages the redistribution of the people's wealth. As the *New York Times* columnist Ross Douthat noted, "The most pernicious sort of redistribution...[is] from savers to speculators, from outsiders to insiders, and from the industrious middle class to the reckless, unproductive rich."[10] It is time to put an end to this most inequitable redistribution of wealth from the productive sector to the overpaid, benefits-rich, bossy bureaucrats. It's time for a citizen revolution to deprive the robber barons of the source of their revenue and power—excessive taxation and excessive government. Bureaucracy is the enemy, rebuilding self-reliance is the goal. And who knows, if we win, we might then all be able to afford a house like Al Gore's.

ACKNOWLEDGMENTS

I'd like first of all to thank my CEI colleagues for their help, suggestions, and input into this book: Fred Smith, Wayne Crews, Sam Kazman, Myron Ebell, all the staff of the Center for Economic Freedom, and my excellent interns Roger Abbott and Dennis Grabowski. The union chapter in particular would not have been possible without the hard work and help of Vinnie Vernuccio and Ivan Osorio. It's as much their chapter as it is mine. Fred especially would appreciate donations to CEI to keep work like this going!

A special thank you goes to Pete Sepp of that crusading group, the National Taxpayers' Union, without whose help the IRS chapter could not have been written. Other thanks go to all the many authors, reporters, and researchers mentioned in this book. I stand on the shoulders of giants.

Further thanks must go to Harry Crocker and Mary Beth Baker for exemplary patience while editing my unwieldy prose.

I'd also like to thank Rich Lowry of *National Review*, Wlady Pleszc-zynski of the *American Spectator*, David Mastio of the *Washington Times*, and Mark Tapscott of the *Washington Examiner* for believing in me and giving me platforms to air some of the ideas contained in this book.

Finally, I'd like to thank my children, Helen and George, for putting up with their daddy going AWOL at weekends while he was writing this book, and to my wife Kristen for providing unfaltering love and support when my faith wavered—and for putting up with the children while I was AWOL. Show your support for Kristen by reading her blog: shoutfirst.blogspot.com!

NOTES

Chapter One

1. Bill Clinton, *My Life* (New York: Random House, Inc., 2004).
2. Andy Barr, "Washington area tops list For income," *The Hill*, February 27, 2006, http://thehill.com/homenews/news/10308-washington-area-tops-list-for-income (accessed March 21, 2011).
3. Julia O'Donoghue, Coming to Our Census: Population Growth, *Fairfax Station–Clifton Connection*, March 3, 2010, http://www.connectionnewspapers.com/article.asp?article=338351&paper=81&cat=104 (accessed March 21, 2011).
4. County of Fairfax, Virginia, Comprehensive Annual Financial Report For Fiscal Year Ending June 30, 2009.
5. Tim Iacono, "There's One Housing Market Is Holding Onto Its Bubble Gains Better Than Any Other," *Business Insider*, November 30, 2010, http://www.businessinsider.com/which-housing-market-is-holding-onto-bubble-gains-better-than-any-other-2010-11 (accessed March 21, 2011).

6.   Jody Shenn, "Fannie Mae and Freddie Mac CEOs' salaries may top $6 million for 2009," Bloomberg News, December 24, 2009, http://www. bloomberg.com/apps/news?pid=newsarchive&sid=ad2b8bETXV8s (accessed March 21, 2011).

7.   Something about which I have grown increasingly skeptical over the years…

8.   Walter Olson, "Rise of an Imperial City, Contd.," Cato Institute, December 9, 2010, http://www.cato-at-liberty.org/rise-of-an-imperial-city-contd/ (accessed March 25, 2010).

9.   Carole Murello and Dan Keating, "Number of black D.C. residents plummets as majority status slips away," *Washington Post,* March 25, 2011, http://www. washingtonpost.com/local/black-dc-residents-plummet-barely-a-majority/2011/03/24/ABtIgJQB_story.html?hpid=z2 (accessed March 25, 2011).

10.   Affidavit of Wendy H. Munoz in support of criminal complaints, http:// www.baltimoresun.com/news/maryland/bal-complaint-johnsons-pdf,0,5023790.htmlpage (accessed December 1, 2010).

11.   "FOX 5 Investigates: Caught on Camera," November 17, 2010, video and transcript at http://www.myfoxdc.com/dpp/news/investigative/fox-5-investigates-caught-on-camera-111710 (accessed March 21, 2011).

Chapter Two

1.   Yes, the Act literally has no name. Its short title is the "_____ Act Of ____" HR 1586 of the 111th Congress—look it up!

2.   Scott McCabe, "D.C. firefighter paid $140,000 to not work," *Washington Examiner,* December 8, 2010, http://washingtonexaminer.com/blogs/capital-land/2010/12/dc-firefighter-paid-14000-not-work (accessed March 25, 2011).

3.   Maria Cramer and Matt Carroll, "Amid cuts, big pay for police," *Boston Globe,* May 6, 2010, http://www.boston.com/news/local/massachusetts/articles/2010/05/06/police_pay_can_exceed_250k/ (accessed March 25, 2011).

4.   Mark Flatten, "Undisciplined Bureaucracy: Civil Service Job Protections Make Disciplining a Problem Government Employee Complicated, Costly and Time-Consuming," Special Investigation No. 10-02, Goldwater Institute, December 8, 2010, www.goldwaterinstitute.org/file/5485/download/5487 (accessed March 24, 2011).

5.   John Derbyshire, "Public vs. Private," National Review Online *The Corner,* September 24, 2009, http://www.nationalreview.com/corner/187654/public-vs-private/john-derbyshire (accessed March 25, 2011).

6. The OMB and CBO have different ways of scoring expenditure, so not all the figures will match.

7. Thanks to Amit Agarwal, "Visualizing a Trillion: Just How Big That Number Is?" Digital Inspiration, September 3, 2009, http://www.labnol. org/internet/visualize-numbers-how-big-is-trillion-dollars/7814/ (accessed March 21, 2011) for these examples.

8. See what I mean when I say pork is not the problem?

9. Editorial, "Gov't Dependents: The New Majority," *Investor's Business Daily*, March 1, 2010, http://www.investors.com/NewsAndAnalysis/ Article.aspx?id=522584 (accessed March 25, 2011).

10. Actually, in some cases they would be doing the work anyway, because taxpayer funding "crowds out" private funding—see chapter six. But that just makes the fact that you have to pay for them doubly insulting!

11. Paul C. Light, "The New True Size of Government," NYU Robert F. Wagner Graduate School of Public Service, Organizational Performance Initiative Research Brief No. 2, 2006.

12. 2009 Annual Survey of State and Local Government Employment and Payroll.

13. As of April 2011, the civilian labor force was 153 million Americans. Add back in the military of 2.2 million, and we get 155 million, which barely changes the proportion." Source: Bureau of Labor Statistics, http://www. bls.gov/news.release/empsit.t01.htm (accessed May 9, 2011).

14. Actually, it could be more than that. In his first press conference in 2009, Secretary of Agriculture Tom Vilsack said he didn't know how many people the USDA employed: "They could tell me how many checks are issued, but not how many people work here. It was the first question I asked the transition staff when the president nominated me for this position. I was interested to know how many people actually work at USDA. And I was told that no one knows for sure."

15. RA-10, "Final Investigation Report Involving Dr. Michael E. Mann," The Pennsylvania State University, June 4, 2010, http://live.psu.edu/fullimg/ userpics/10026/Final_Investigation_Report.pdf (accessed March 21, 2011).

16. Eric Mar, biography City and County of San Francisco Board of Supervisors website: http://www.sfbos.org/index.aspx?page=2083 (accessed March 21, 2011).

17. Heather Knight, "3 S.F. school board members accused of plot on Ackerman," *San Francisco Chronicle*, September 24, 2003.

Chapter Three

1.   "Historical Documents relating to Alphonse (Al) Capone, Chicago," IRS.
      gov, http://www.irs.gov/foia/article/0,,id=179352,00.html (accessed March
      21, 2011).
2.   US Census Bureau, Statistical Abstract of the United States, 2011, Table
      700.
3.   Bureau of Labor Statistics, Occupational Outlook Handbook 2010-11,
      http://www.bls.gov/oco/ocos260.htm (accessed March 21, 2011).
4.   Scott A. Hodge, J. Scott Moody, and Wendy P. Warcholik, Ph.D., The
      Rising Cost of Complying with the Federal Income Tax, Tax Foundation
      Special Report No. 138, January 10, 2006.
5.   Chris Edwards, "Top Ten Civil Liberties Abuses of the Income Tax," *Tax
      & Budget Bulletin* No. 4, Cato Institute, April 2002, http://www.cato.org/
      pubs/tbb/tbb-0204-2.html (accessed March 21, 2011).
6.   Joe Nocera, "In Prison for Taking a Liar Loan," *New York Times*, March
      25, 2011, http://www.nytimes.com/2011/03/26/business/26nocera.htm
      (accessed March 28, 2011).
7.   Tim Carney, "GE's 900 tax experts—How big government is ruining
      America," *Washington Examiner*, March 25, 2011, http://washingtonex-
      aminer.com/blogs/beltway-confidential/2011/03/ges-900-tax-experts-how-
      big-government-ruining-america#ixzz1Hv259Byn (accessed March 28,
      2011).
8.   Sheri Falk, "Filing Your Taxes is Getting Easier," WDAM.com, undated
      2011, http://www.wdam.com/Global/story.asp?S=14308792 (accessed
      March 24, 2011).
9.   Dan Alban, "The IRS and the Latest Licensing Outrage," *The Daily Caller*,
      October 8, 2010, http://dailycaller.com/2010/10/08/the-irs-and-the-latest-
      licensing-outrage/ (accessed March 24, 2011).
10.   Neil DeMause, "Health care law's massive, hidden tax change,"
      CNNMoney.com, May 5, 2010, http://money.cnn.com/2010/05/05/small-
      business/1099_health_care_tax_change/ (accessed March 21, 2011).
11.   The Editors, "The 1099 Insurrection," *Wall Street Journal*, September 15,
      2010, http://online.wsj.com/article/SB10001424052748703897204575
      4882726915140740000.html (accessed March 21, 2011).
12.   The Editors, "The 1099 Repudiation," *Wall Street Journal*, February 5,
      2011, http://online.wsj.com/article/SB10001424052748704709304576
      124090853943176.html (accessed March 21, 2011).

Chapter Four

1.   You can download the declassified manual at http://svn.cacert.org/CAcert/CAcert_Inc/Board/oss/OSS_Simple_Sabotage_Manual.pdf (accessed March 23, 2011).

2.   Barack Obama, "Toward a 21st-Century Regulatory System: If the FDA deems saccharin safe enough for coffee, then the EPA should not treat it as hazardous waste," *Wall Street Journal*, January 18, 2010, http://online.wsj.com/article/SB10001424052748703396604576088272112103698.html (accessed March 23, 2011).

3.   George Allen and Marlo Lewis, "Overturning EPA's Endangerment Finding is a Constitutional Imperative," CEI OnPoint No. 167, May 19, 2010, http://cei.org/sites/default/files/Marlo%20Lewis%20-%20Overturning%20EPA's%20Endangerment%20Finding%20-%20FINAL,%20May%2019,%202010,%20PDF.pdf (accessed March 23, 2011).

4.   W. Mark Crain, "The Impact of Regulatory Costs on Small Firms," Small Business Administration Office of Advocacy, September 2005, http://archive.sba.gov/advo/research/rs264tot.pdf (accessed March 23, 2011).

5.   James L. Gattuso, "Red Tape Rising: Regulatory Trends in the Bush Years," Backgrounder No. 2116, Heritage Foundation, March 25, 2008, http://s3.amazonaws.com/thf_media/2008/pdf/bg2116.pdf (accessed March 23, 2011).

6.   Andrew M. Langer, "The Context of Regulation: Reducing the Incremental Costs," Testimony submitted to the U.S. Senate Committee on Small Business, Hearing on Small Business Regulatory Burdens, November 18, 2010.

7.   Larry J. Sabato, *PAC Power: Inside the World of Political Action Committees* (New York: W. W. Norton 1984).

8.   Chris Horner, "Zoi-ks!" *American Spectator*, October 13, 2010, http://spectator.org/blog/2010/10/13/zoi-ks (accessed April 1, 2011).

9.   Tim Carney, "Bail them out, regulate them, then work for them," *Washington Examiner*, January 19, 2011, http://washingtonexaminer.com/politics/2011/01/bail-them-out-regulate-them-then-work-them (accessed March 23, 2011).

10. Promontory Financial Group press release, "Amy Friend, Former Chief Counsel of Senate Banking Committee, Joins Promontory as a Managing Director," Washington, D.C., January 17, 2010, http://www.promontory.com/assets/0/78/108/120/31ad02c2-d18e-4880-b509-8fc9b95dad19.pdf (accessed March 23, 2011).

11. Michael Fumento, "Toyota Hysteria: Horror Stories Really About Us," *New York Post*, March 16, 2010.

12.   Michael Fumento, "Toyota Hybrid Horror Hoax," Forbes Online, March 12, 2010, http://www.forbes.com/2010/03/12/toyota-autos-hoax-media-opinions-contributors-michael-fumento.html (accessed March 23, 2011).

13.   Mike Ramsey and Josh Mitchell, "Release of Toyota Documents Blocked, Ex-Official Says," *Wall Street Journal*, July 30, 2010, http://online.wsj.com/article/SB10001424052748703999304575399523349443634.html (accessed March 23, 2011).

14.   Associated Press, "Toyota trying to move beyond safety concerns," February 9, 2011.

Chapter Five

1.   Daarel Burnette II, "In St Paul schools, the not so sweet life," *Star Tribune*, December 22, 2010, http://www.startribune.com/local/stpaul/112131574.html (accessed March 22, 2011).

2.   Arun Gupta, "How TV Superchef Jamie Oliver's 'Food Revolution' Flunked Out," AlterNet, April 8, 2010, http://www.alternet.org/story/146354/how_tv_superchef_jamie_oliver's_'food_revolution'_flunked_out?page=entire (accessed March 22, 2011).

3.   Phebe Phillips, "Everything is Perfect…I Changed!" College of Arts and Sciences of Texas Women's University, transcript of commencement address, May 14, 2010, http://phebephillips.com/pdf/PhebePhillips-TWU-Commencement-Address.pdf (accessed March 22, 2011).

4.   Jayne O'Donnell, "Lead testing can be costly for mom and pop toy shops," *USA Today*, June 17, 2010, http://www.usatoday.com/money/industries/retail/2010-06-17-productsafety17_ST_N.htm (accessed March 22, 2011).

5.   Rick Woldenberg, "CPSIA – Casualty of the Week for June 1," Amend the CPSIA, June 3, 2010, http://amendthecpsia.com/2010/06/cpsia-casualty-of-the-week-for-june-1/ (accessed March 22, 2011).

6.   Rick Woldenberg, "GUEST BLOG – Jolie Fay's Story," Amend the CPSIA, July 14, 2010, http://amendthecpsia.com/2010/07/guest-blog-jolie-fays-story/ (accessed March 22, 2011).

7.   Letter from Anne M. Northrop, Commissioner U.S. Consumer Product Safety Commission, to The Honorable Henry Waxman, Chairman Committee on Energy and Commerce, March 18, 2010, http://www.cpsc.gov/pr/northup03182010.pdf (accessed April 1, 2011).

8.   The CPSIA story lumbers on. If you want to follow the unfolding saga, there is no better place than Walter Olson's Overlawyered.com.

9.   Garrett A. Vaughn, "Clearing the Air on the EPA's False Regulatory Benefit-Cost Estimates and Its Anti-Carbon Agenda," CEI *On Point* No. 173,

Competitive Enterprise Institute, March 17, 2011, http://cei.org/sites/default/files/Garrett%20Vaughn%20-%20Clearing%20the%20Air.pdf (accessed March 25, 2011).

10. Randal Lutter and Richard B. Belzer, "EPA Pats Itself on the Back," *Regulation*, Vol. 23 no.3, http://www.cato.org/pubs/regulation/regv23n3/lutter.pdf (accessed March 25, 2011).

Chapter Six

1. Larry Greenemeier, "Exposing the Weakest Link: As Airline Passenger Security Tightens, Bombers Target Cargo Holds," *Scientific American*, November 2, 2010, http://www.scientificamerican.com/article.cfm?id=aircraft-cargo-bomb-security (accessed March 24, 2011).

2. Becky Akers, "A better way than the TSA," *Christian Science Monitor*, March 21, 2007, http://www.csmonitor.com/2007/0321/p09s01-coop.html (accessed March 24, 2011).

3. Thomas Frank, "Most fake bombs missed by screeners," *USA Today*, October 18, 2007, http://www.usatoday.com/travel/news/2007-10-17-airport-security_N.htm (accessed March 24, 2011).

4. Deborah Sherman and Dan Weaver, "Undercover agents slip bombs past DIA screeners," CBS 9News.com, date unverifiable 2007, http://www.9news.com/news/article.aspx?storyid=67166

5. Catherine Rampell, "Ex-employee says FAA warned before 9/11," *USA Today*, November 24, 2006, http://www.usatoday.com/news/washington/2006-11-23-whistle-blower-faa_x.htm (accessed March 24, 2011).

6. Iain Murray, "For the TSA, all risks are created equal," Competitive Enterprise Institute, originally published in The Star Telegram, December 25, 2010, http://cei.org/op-eds-articles/tsa-all-risks-are-created-equal (accessed May 17, 2011).

7. Terence Kealey, *The Economic Laws of Scientific Research* (New York: St. Martin's Press, 1996), 7–8.

8. Edwin Mansfield, "Academic Research and Industrial Innovation," *Research Policy*, 20 (1991), pp. 1–12; Gellman Associates, Indicators of International Trends in Technological Innovation, Report to the National Science foundation (Washington, D.C., 1976); E. Mansfield, "Basic Research and Productivity Increase in Manufacturing," American Economic Review, 70 (1980), 141–54; Z. Griliches, "Productivity, R&D and Basic Research at the Firm Level in the 1970s," *American Economic Review*, 76 (1986), 141–54.

9.   Timothy Pigford, et al., v. Dan Glickman, Secretary, United States Depart-
      ment of Agriculture, U.S. District Court for the District of Columbia, Civil
      Action No. 97-1978 (PLF). Paul L. Friedman, U.S. District Judge.

10.   Tadlock Cowan and Jody Feder, "The Pigford Cases: USDA Settlement of
      Discrimination Suits by Black Farmers," CRS Report for Congress, Decem-
      ber 10, 2010, http://www.nationalaglawcenter.org/assets/crs/RS20430.pdf
      (accessed March 24, 2011).

11.   Diane Dahle, "Pigford Settlement," Cause of Liberty blog, December 14,
      2010, http://causeofliberty.blogspot.com/2010/12/pigford-settlement.html
      (accessed March 24, 2011).

12.   Tommy Christopher, "Andrew Breitbart Re-Addresses Shirley Sherrod And
      The Pigford Settlement," MediaIte.com, October 6, 2010, http://www.
      mediaite.com/online/andrew-breitbart-re-addresses-shirley-sherrod-and-
      the-pigford-settlement/ (accessed March 24, 2011).

13.   Ibid.

14.   Andrew Breitbart, "Left, Right and Pigford: Introducing Lee Stranahan-
      BigGovernment.com's 'Progressive' Pigford Film Documentarian," Big-
      Government.com, December 19, 2010, http://biggovernment.com/
      abreitbart/2010/12/19/left-right-and-pigford-introducing-lee-stranahan-
      biggovernment-coms-progressive-pigford-film-documentarian/ (accessed
      March 24, 2011).

15.   Lee Stranahan, "Pigford Video Blockbuster: Key 'Black Farmers' Lawyer
      Admits Clients 'Got Away With Murder,'" BigJournalism.com, December
      19, 2010, http://bigjournalism.com/lstranahan/2010/12/19/pigford-video-
      blockbuster-key-black-farmers-lawyer-admits-clients-got-away-with-
      murder/#more-151272 (accessed March 24, 2011).

16.   Ibid.

17.   Lucia Graves, "House Republicans Allege Fraud In Settlement With Black
      Farmers, Call For Investigation," *Huffington Post*, September 29, 2010,
      http://www.huffingtonpost.com/2010/09/29/black-farmers-settlement-
      fraud-allegations_n_744439.html (accessed March 24, 2011).

18.   Editorial, "USDA's Pigford fraud," *Washington Times*, February 2,
      2011.

19.   Executive Office of the President, Budget of the United States Government:
      Historical Tables, 2006.

20.   USDA, Budget Summary and Annual Performance Plan, Financial Year 2012.

21.   Gerald P. O'Driscoll Jr., "The Gulf Spill, the Financial Crisis and Govern-
      ment Failure," *Wall Street Journal*, June 12, 2010.

Chapter Seven

1.   Address delivered to the Council of Foreign Relations, New York City, December 10, 1918, *American Federationist*, February 1919, p. 160

2.   Annais Morales, John Doyle and Leonard Green, "Storm's Baby Nightmare," *New York Post*, December 31, 2010. http://www.nypost.com/p/news/local/queens/storm_baby_nightmare_Aq85Gkd6KdoieXPnP4ECJN#ixzz1AAwzNtox (accessed March 24, 2011).

3.   Sally Goldenberg, John Doyle, and Josh Margolin, "Sanitation Workers Targeted Specific Neighborhoods," *New York Post*, December 31, 2010, http://www.nypost.com/p/news/local/sanit_put_key_hoods_on_ice_WzL-VUKqeHesqHTCHpR6BcP (accessed March 24, 2011).

4.   Ibid

5.   Ibid

6.   Top Industries Giving to Members of Congress, 2010 cycle, Opensecrets.org, http://www.opensecrets.org/industries/mems.php (accessed May 9, 2011).

7.   Ivan Osorio, Administration Keeping Cozy with Union Bosses, *The Daily Caller*, March 1, 2010, http://dailycaller.com/2010/03/01/administration-keeping-cozy-with-union-bosses/ (accessed March 24, 2011).

8.   James Sherk, "Inflated Federal Pay: How Americans Are Overtaxed to Overpay the Civil Service," Center for Data Analysis Report #10-05, The Heritage Foundation, July 7, 2010, http://www.heritage.org/research/reports/2010/07/inflated-federal-pay-how-americans-are-overtaxed-to-overpay-the-civil-service (accessed March 24, 2011).

9.   Chris Edwards, "Federal Pay Outpaces Private Sector Pay," *Tax and Budget Bulletin* No. 35, Cato Institute, May 2006, http://www.cato.org/pubs/tbb/tbb-0605-35.pdf (accessed March 24, 2011).

10.   Terry Moe, "Political Control and the Power of the Agent," *Journal of Law, Economics, and Organization*. Vol. 22, No. 1 (Spring): 1-29, 2006.

11.   Tim Pawlenty, "Government Unions vs. Taxpayers," *Wall Street Journal*, December 13, 2010, http://online.wsj.com/article/SB10001424052748703766704576009350303578410.html (accessed March 24, 2011).

12.   F. Vincent Vernuccio, "Federal workers will still receive raises despite pay freeze," *The Daily Caller*, December 2, 2010, http://dailycaller.com/2010/12/02/federal-workers-will-still-receive-raises-despite-pay-freeze/ (accessed March 24, 2011).

13.   Dennis Cauchon, "For feds, more get 6-figure salaries," *USA Today*, December 11, 2009, http://www.usatoday.com/news/washington/2009-12-10-federal-pay-salaries_N.htm (accessed March 24, 2011).

14. Gordon Tullock, Economic Hierarchies, Organization and the Structure of Production, Kluwer Academic Publishers, 1992.

15. Ibid.

16. Jason Stein and Patrick Marley, "Walker budget plan would limit state unions to negotiating only on salaries," JSOnline.com, February 10, 2011, http://www.jsonline.com/news/statepolitics/115726754.html (accessed March 31, 2011).

17. Jim Siegel, "Collective bargaining protestors, supporters clash at state-house," *Columbus Dispatch*, February 17, 2011, http://www.dispatch.com/live/content/local_news/stories/2011/02/17/collective-bargaining-supporters-protestors-clash-at-statehouse.html (accessed March 28 2011).

18. Chas Sisk, "TN Republicans back off teacher collective bargaining ban," *The Tennessean*, March 17, 2011, http://www.wbir.com/news/article/162107/2/TN-Republicans-back-off-teacher-collective-bargaining-ban (accessed March 28, 2011).

19. F. Vincent Vernuccio, "United Auto Workers Local Costs 650 Jobs in Indi-ana," Townhall.com, September 29, 2010, http://townhall.com/columnists/vincentvernuccio/2010/09/29/united_auto_workers_local_costs_650_jobs_in_indiana (accessed March 24, 2011).

Chapter Eight

1. "Controller: $2.19 billion in California bills may go unpaid without bud-get," *Los Angeles Times*, August 3, 2010, http://latimesblogs.latimes.com/california-politics/2010/08/more-than-2-billion-in-california-bills-may-go-unpaid-without-budget.html (accessed March 31, 2011).

2. Steven Greenhut, "Class War: How Public Servants Became Our Masters," *Reason*, February 2010, http://reason.com/archives/2010/01/12/class-war (accessed March 28, 2011).

3. Elisa Hahn, "Family charged 'death tax' for baby who lived one hour," King5.com, January 10, 2011, http://www.king5.com/news/local/Family-charged-with-death-tax-for-baby-who-lives-one-hour-113256474.html (accessed March 31, 2011).

4. "Berkeley Postpones Vote on Taxpayer-Funded Sex Change Operations," sanfrancisco.cbslocal.com, January 18, 2010, http://sanfrancisco.cbslocal.com/2011/01/18/berkeley-to-vote-on-taxpayer-funded-sex-change-operations/ (accessed March 31, 2011).

5. Associated Press, "Budget Cuts To Darken SoCal City Street Lights," December 20, 2010.

6. Jeff Gottlieb and Ruben Vives, "Is a City Manager Worth $800,000 a Year?" *Los Angeles Times*, July 12, 2010, http://articles.latimes.com/2010/jul/15/local/la-me-bell-salary-20100715 (accessed March 31, 2011).

7.   Associated Press, "Los Angeles suburb residents march over high city salaries," July 25, 2010.

8.   Jeff Gottlieb and Ruben Vives, "Bell councilman 'ashamed,' 'disgusted' that Rizzo earned $1.5 million," *Los Angeles Times*, August 8, 2010, http://articles.latimes.com/2010/aug/08/local/la-me-bell-manager-compensation-mobile (accessed March 31, 2011).

9.   Jack Leonard, Andrew Blankstein, and Jeff Gottlieb, "In e-mails, Bell official discussed fat salaries," *Los Angeles Times*, February 14, 2011, http://articles.latimes.com/2011/feb/14/local/la-me-bell-emails-20110215 (accessed March 31, 2011).

10. "3 accused Bell officials want cash-strapped city to pay their legal bills," KLA 5 News, San Diego, January 11, 2011, http://latimesblogs.latimes.com/lanow/2011/01/accused-bell-officials-want-cash-strapped-city-to-pay-their-legal-bills.html (accessed March 31, 2011).

11. Don Bellante, David Denholm, and Ivan G. Osorio, "Vallejo Con Dios: Why Public Sector Unionism Is a Bad Deal for Taxpayers and Representative Government," Policy Analysis No. 645, The Cato Institute, September 28, 2009, http://www.cato.org/pub_display.php?pub_id=10569 (accessed March 31, 2011).

12. Steven Greenhut, *Plunder! How Public Employee Unions are Raiding Treasuries, Controlling Our Lives and Bankrupting the Nation* (Santa Ana, CA: The Forum Press, 2009).

13. Michael M. Grynbaum, "$239,000 Conductor Among M.T.A.'s 8,000 Six-Figure Workers," *New York Times*, June 2, 2010, http://www.nytimes.com/2010/06/03/nyregion/03mta.html?_r=1 (accessed March 31, 2011).

14. Kathy Curran, "I-Team: State Employees Given Months of Vacation Time," WBZ-TV, November 22, 2010, http://boston.cbslocal.com/2010/11/22/i-team-state-employees-given-months-of-vacation-time/ (accessed March 31, 2011).

15. Carl Campanile, "Suspended PA cops still scoring overtime pay," *New York Post*, June 21, 2010, http://www.nypost.com/p/news/local/suspended_pa_cops_still_scoring_Xle4nA3wGvbOqCDOVj5TiL (accessed March 31, 2011).

16. WRAL news, "Audit: Durham police chief dismissed overtime concerns," WRAL.com, September 9, 2009, http://www.wral.com/news/local/wral_investigates/story/6106833/ (accessed March 31, 2011).

17. Maria Cramer and Matt Carroll, "Amid cuts, big pay for police," *Boston Globe*, May 6, 2010, http://www.boston.com/news/local/massachusetts/articles/2010/05/06/police_pay_can_exceed_250k/ (accessed March 28, 2011).

18. Ryan O'Johnston, "Boston Police Department brass ignored 2001 audit of OT: No probe after 400 apparent violations," *Boston Herald*, March

24, 2011, http://news.bostonherald.com/news/regional/
view/2011_0324bpd_brass_ignored_01_audit_of_ot_no_probe_
after_400_apparent_violations/ (accessed March 28, 2011).

19. John Derbyshire, "The USA's Very Own Greece Problem," National Review
     Online *The Corner*, February 15, 2010, http://www.nationalreview.com/
     corner/194867/u-s-s-very-own-greece-problem/john-derbyshire (accessed
     March 25, 2011).

Chapter Nine

1.   David M. Herzenhorn, "First Lady Campaigns for Teachers and Trainees,"
     New York Times, September 3, 2003, http://www.nytimes.com/2003/09/03/
     nyregion/first-lady-campaigns-for-teachers-and-trainees.html?src=pm
     (accessed March 31, 2011).

2.   Aaron Smith, "Teachers give job prospects an 'F'," CNNmoney.com, May
     9, 2008, http://money.cnn.com/2008/05/07/news/economy/teacher/index.
     htm (accessed March 31, 2011).

3.   Richard Cohen, "Leave No Teacher Behind," *Washington Post*, November
     18, 2003, http://www.washingtonpost.com/ac2/wp-dyn/A54785-
     2003Nov17?language=printer (accessed March 31, 2011).

4.   American Federation of Teachers, "Survey and Analysis of Teacher Salary
     Trends 2007," AFT 2008, http://www.aft.org/pdfs/teachers/salarysurvey07.
     pdf (accessed March 31, 2011).

5.   Jay P. Greene and Marcus A. Winters, "How Much Are Public School Teach-
     ers Paid?" *Civic Report* No. 50, Manhattan Institute, January 2007, http://
     www.manhattan-institute.org/html/cr_50.htm (accessed March 31, 2011).

6.   Jay P. Greene and Marcus A. Winters, "Is $34.06 Per Hour 'Underpaid'?"
     Wall Street Journal, February 2, 2007.

7.   Joel Klein, "Why Teacher Pensions Don't Work," *Wall Street Journal*,
     January 11, 2011, http://online.wsj.com/article/SB100014240527487044
     15104576066192958395176.html (accessed March 31, 2011).

8.   Jason Felch, Jason Song, and Doug Smith, "When layoffs come to LA
     schools, performance doesn't count," *Los Angeles Times*, December 4,
     2010, http://articles.latimes.com/2010/dec/04/local/la-me-1205-teachers-
     seniority-20101204 (accessed March 31, 2011).

9.   Editorial, "Largess for Loudoun Teachers," *Washington Post*, November 25,
     2010, http://www.washingtonpost.com/wp-dyn/content/article/2010/11/25/
     AR2010112502738.html (accessed March 31, 2011).

10. Karen Matthews, "700 NYC Teachers Are Paid to Do Nothing," Associ-
     ated Press, June 22, 2009.

11. Ellen Ishkanian, "Wellesley School Budget: Library, Art, Music and Phys Ed Eyed for Cuts," *Wellesley Patch*, January 19, 2011, http://wellesley. patch.com/articles/library-art-music-and-phys-ed-eyed-for-wellesley-school-budget-cuts (accessed March 31, 2011).

12. Bob Wheaton, "39 school employees in area make more than $100,000; Jackson Public Schools had 16 on list," *Jackson Citizen Patriot*, October 16, 2010.

13. Brad Lips and Evan Feinberg, "The Administrative Burden of No Child Left Behind," The Heritage Foundation, March 23, 2007, http://www. heritage.org/research/reports/2007/03/the-administrative-burden-of-no-child-left-behind?renderforprint=1 (accessed March 31, 2011).

14. General Accountability Office, "Education Finance: The Extent of Federal Funding in State Education Agencies," GAO/HEHS-95-3, October 1994.

15. "NCLB Costs," State Reports, Communities for Quality Education, http:// www.qualityednow.org/research/nclb-costs.php (accessed March 31, 2011).

16. "Are High School Grades Inflated?" Issues in College Readiness, IC 050805240, ACT 2005, http://www.act.org/research/policymakers/pdf/ issues.pdf (accessed March 31, 2011).

17. Eleanor Chute, "In high schools, a 'B' is new 'C'," *Pittsburgh Post-Gazette*, June 3, 2007, http://www.post-gazette.com/pg/07154/791202-298.stm (accessed March 31, 2011).

18. Justin Pope, "Admissions Boards Face 'Grade Inflation'," Associated Press, November 18, 2006.

19. Justin Pope, "Rising GPAs make it harder to get into college," Associated Press, November 18, 2006, http://www.usatoday.com/news/ education/2006-11-18-school-grades_x.htm (accessed March 28, 2011).

20. Stuart Rojstaczer, "Where All Grades Are Above Average," *Washington Post*, January 28, 2003, http://www.washingtonpost.com/ac2/wp-dyn?pagename=article&contentId=A52648-2003Jan27&notFound=true (accessed March 31, 2011).

21. Thomas Reeves, "The Happy Classroom: Grade Inflation Works," National Association of Scholars, April 16, 2009, http://www.nas.org/ polArticles.cfm?doc_id=708 (accessed March 31, 2011).

22. "Visualizing the U.S. Higher Education Bubble," *Seeking Alpha*, September 8, 2010, http://seekingalpha.com/article/224333-visualizing-the-u-s-higher-education-bubble (accessed March 31, 2011).

23. Glenn Reynolds, "Higher education's bubble is about to burst," *Washington Examiner*, June 6, 2010, http://washingtonexaminer.com/node/80276 (accessed March 31, 2011).

24.   Lisa Rein and Ed O'Keefe, "New Post poll finds negativity towards federal workers," *Washington Post*, October 18, 2011, http://www.washingtonpost. com/wp-dyn/content/article/2010/10/17/AR2010101703866. html?sid=ST2010101703889 (accessed March 25, 2011).

25.   Calculations by Visible Economy LLC – see Mike Mandel, "Where Young College Grads Are Finding Jobs: Government," http://innovationandgrowth. wordpress.com/2010/10/05/where-young-college-grads-are-finding-jobs-government/ (accessed March 31, 2011).

Conclusion

1.   Mona Charen, "Abolishing the Department of Education isn't Extreme," *Washington Examiner*, June 13, 2010, http://washingtonexaminer.com/ node/77401 (accessed March 25, 2011).

2.   Nick Gillespie and Veronique de Rugy, "The 19 Percent Solution," *Reason*, March 2011, http://reason.com/archives/2011/02/14/the-19-percent-solution (accessed March 25, 2011).

3.   See the Roadmap to America's Future at http://www.roadmap.republicans. budget.house.gov/Plan/#Healthsecurity (accessed March 25, 2011).

4.   Robert H. Frank, "The Other Milton Friedman: A Conservative With a Social Welfare Program," *New York Times*, November 23 2006, http://www. nytimes.com/2006/11/23/business/23scene.html (accessed March 25, 2011).

5.   Wayne Crews and Ryan Young, "Six Painless Ways to Cut Federal Red Tape," AOL News, January 19, 2011, http://www.aolnews.com/2011/01/19/ opinion-6-painless-ways-to-cut-federal-red-tape/ (accessed March 25, 2011).

6.   James Sherk, "What Do Union Members Want? What Paycheck Protection Laws Show About How Well Unions Reflect Their Members' Priorities," Heritage Foundation Center for Data Analysis, August 30, 2006.

7.   For more on this idea see Virginia Postrel, "Unions Forever?" *Reason*, May 1998, http://reason.com/archives/1998/05/01/unions-forever (accessed March 25, 2011).

8.   Steven Greenhut cites this example in his book, *Plunder! How Public Employee Unions are Raiding Treasuries, Controlling Our Lives and Bankrupting the Nation* (Santa Ana, CA: The Forum Press, 2009).

9.   Muninet, "Trends Point to Neighborhood Privatization," September 25, 2007, http://www.muninetguide.com/articles/Trend-Points-to-Neighborhood-Pri-244.php (accessed March 25, 2011).

10.   Ross Douthat, "The Class War We Need," *New York Times*, July 11, 2010, http://www.nytimes.com/2010/07/12/opinion/12douthat.html (accessed March 25, 2011).

INDEX

205